DAVID A. STOOP

ways to help them learn
youth · grades 7 to 12

G/L REGAL BOOKS

INTERNATIONAL CENTER FOR LEARNING

A Division of G/L Publications, Glendale, California, U. S. A.

CONTENTS

PREFACE

Training materials for use with this handbook are available from your church supplier.

THE AUTHOR

David A. Stoop graduated from Stetson University and is continuing graduate study at Fuller Theological Seminary.

Mr. Stoop's ministry includes eleven years of working particularly with youth on the east and west coasts. He has served in Christian Missionary Alliance and Evangelical Covenant churches in Florida and California. His personal study and experience in creatively guiding Bible study groups of youth and adults has equipped him to handle free-lance writing assignments for G/L Youth Division publications.

Since the manuscript for this book was completed, Dave has joined the staff of G/L Publications as Editor in the Adult Department.

Dave and Jan Stoop are the parents of three boys.

The late Dr. Henrietta C. Mears, founder of Gospel Light Publications and distinguished Christian education leader for more than 40 years, often said, "Good teachers are not born; they are made by conscientious labor." It is axiomatic that if one is to be successful in any field, he must be trained. Our Lord recognized this fact in training the Twelve. First He spent the whole night in prayer in preparation for the momentous task of choosing them. From this point the teaching and training of these men became a matter of paramount importance to Him.

A tremendous passion for the training of leadership has been a hallmark in the program of Gospel Light. What workers learn today will determine what the church will be tomorrow. This is the great need of the hour; to train leaders for Christian service, and particularly the Sunday school, people who will know how to administer and teach. With a deep sense of obligation as well as opportunity the International Center for Learning was created in 1970 to specialize in the training of dedicated personnel in all departments of the local church.

This is one of a series of textbooks designed to train workers in the Sunday school. It has grown out of actual proven experience and represents the best educational philosophy. In addition to textual materials, the full program of ICL includes audio visual media and church leadership training seminars sponsored in strategic centers across America and ultimately overseas as rapidly as God enables. We are being deluged with requests to help in the momentous task of training workers. We dare not stop short of providing all possible assistance.

Train for Sunday school success! Train for church growth! Train people by example and experience to pray and plan and perform. Christ trained the Twelve. Dare we do less?

Cyrus N. Nelson
President, Gospel Light Publications

PART I

YOUTH—THEIR CULTURE

Young people are getting excited about Jesus Christ. They are coming alive for Him! Is the Sunday school youth department helping in any way to encourage and support this reviving wind? Can the Sunday school be a source of motivation for youth to grow and mature in the knowledge of Jesus Christ? Or is it watching the action pass by?

A well-known pastor recently pleaded with his people to pray for revival. His reason? So that adults might show youth what revival is all about. Perhaps the pastor suffered from the same panic expressed by a little figure painted on a coffee mug. He looked confused, and the caption quoted his words: "Where are they? Which way did they go? I'm their leader!" The revival *is* taking place among youth—and the Sunday school can provide leadership and nurture for young Christians.

But the effective Sunday school needs adult leaders who will constantly evaluate what is done and why it is done that way— adult leaders who are concerned about goals and directions that are oriented toward the future and toward Jesus Christ, who is Lord of the future and the *now*.

This manual is designed to assist you in your role as a leader of youth. God grant us all the courage and wisdom to be willing to explore *with* youth the adventure of living in Christ!

CHAPTER ONE

IS THERE *REALLY* A GENERATION GAP?

Today almost any problem arising between youth and adults is quickly diagnosed as a case of "Generation Gapitis." You know how it goes. The discussion ends with the question being hurled at you, "How can you understand? You're from a different generation." Perhaps you've even hesitated to work in the youth department of the church because you fear that the gap is just too wide. The diagnosis of "Generation Gapitis" is not an answer but a cop-out—a way to avoid the problems of communication between adults and adolescents.

But increasingly the very existence of the "generation gap" is being questioned. Is it really any different from the gulf you felt at times between you and *your* parents? Is it really any different from the complaints voiced by Socrates about that unruly generation of young people, who had bad manners, contempt for authority, and disrespect for their elders? More and more, psychologists and sociologists are saying that the idea of a serious generation gap which is unique to our age is really absurd and untrue. It is something that has always existed. There are many references by historians to the complaints of the Egyptians, Greeks and Romans about the problems they had with their youth. Some have suggested that the problem with the prodigal son was a case of "Generation Gapitis." It is not something new to our age.

A close look at the present adolescent generation would reveal that the typical young person holds many of the same liberal or conservative attitudes as his parents. His political views are not really so different from those of his parents. A certain number of youth has always rejected the ideas and attitudes of society, but today the communications media have zeroed in on these young people as though they were representative of the entire younger generation. During the late sixties the term "generation gap" was invented. Since then, television and Madison Avenue have overused and abused the term. This exposure has magnified the problems between generations. As a result, adults pull away from contact with young people, and the problems grow even larger.

At close range, though, there does seem to be a separation between the generations that is much wider than in the past. It goes beyond a mere gap created by age. A 40-year-old has always had a different perspective than a 15-year-old. The difference in years is bound to have an effect on people. But the difference today between the generations is more than just a difference created by age. To understand it, we must take into account some of the differences between the adult culture and the youth culture. We could, in fact, call it a "culture canyon."

WHAT IS A CULTURE CANYON?

A simple definition of culture is: a way of life for a certain group of people. Young people have a way of life that is all theirs. They look at life, understand and interpret it according to their own perspective. Adults, too, have a culture of their own—a special way of life. And today these two cultures are getting farther and farther apart. The culture canyon is beginning to rival the Grand Canyon. It goes far beyond the differences caused by the varied perspectives of age. It even involves different ways of thinking and dealing with "truth."

Why the widening of the canyon between the adult culture and the youth culture?

Probably the most obvious reason is that the present youth generation was raised in a completely different world than the one in which the adult generation was raised. One of the biggest changes involves our means of communication, particularly television. Ross Snyder, in his book on youth culture,[1] points out that the dominant means of communication is one of the most basic forces that shapes people. This especially involves the way they think and the way they interpret life. The present youth generation is the first television generation. They were *raised* on television, whereas adults encountered it later in their lives.

Marshall McLuhan[2] goes so far as to say that we are in a new age: the age of electronic consciousness. We're in a new age because we have a totally new way to communicate. He traces the history of man in three stages. The first is the tribal stage, the age of speech. During this time, all communication was face-to-face. There were no newspapers, books were rare, except in the monastic schools, and only a very few could read. All communication took place within situations. It was a person-to-person means of communicating. Even history was told as the sages would pass on the traditions verbally. Not only was communication limited to the personal method of talking, it was also limited by time and space. Man's world-view was small. It was limited to his tribe, his village, and his age. What took place several hundred miles away never touched him or made any impression on his way of life. There are examples of this even today. Isolated tribes in remote jungles still live in the stone age. In this tribal stage theirs is a small and limited world.

But suddenly a change came. Gutenberg appeared on the scene in the fifteenth century, and with his invention of movable type, he launched the world into stage two—the age of the printed page.

Man's perspective changed abruptly. Unlimited by space and time, man could reach back through the centuries by means of the printed page, and share in the knowledge and wisdom of Plato, Aristotle and countless others. The influence of the past in many different cultures now had an effect on him. Events taking place hundreds of miles away could be preserved in print and delivered to him. The Reformation spread rapidly through manuals and leaflets produced by the printing press. Support for Luther's position was possible because he could appeal to the Scriptures, and people were now able to have their own Bibles. Will Durant points out that the invention of the printing press "paved the way for the Enlightenment, for the American and French revolutions, for democracy."[3] The age of speech was followed by the age of print.

We are still influenced by both modes of communication, and always will be. The spoken word and the printed page are still powerful. But within a lifetime, we have seen the introduction of the third stage in man's history—the age of electronics, primarily television. With the advent of television the world has again shrunk. It is a tribal world again, but this time the whole world is the tribe. The whole globe is a village. The communication-within-the-situation now comes into our living rooms. Whereas in stage one, man was only affected by what happened within a small geographical circle drawn around his tribe and village, man is now affected by what happens around the entire globe.

Here's an illustration. A Sunday school teacher sat in his living room and watched the evening news. All at once he was in the inner city, in the midst of a riot. He saw the rocks come flying toward him and he saw the shotgun blasts. He even flinched as a rock came flying near the television camera. He was involved! He felt as if he were right there! This was part of his village. Then a few moments later he was in Cambodia, watching young Cambodian recruits heading into their first battle. Again, he heard the gunshots. This was real—he saw it happening. He held his breath fearing one of these men might be shot right in front of his eyes. He was again present! He was involved! This was happening "live." He would not have to wait for the morning paper; he was present, watching the news happen in another part of *his village.* Across the top of the television screen came the words "via satellite." Thanks to electronics, he became involved. *The* world is suddenly *his* world.

Now adults and youth as they watch television are both influenced by it. But the adult generation, the adult culture was not shaped and formed by the medium of television. The type of communication that shaped the perspective of the adult culture was a limited one. Radio was informative but not engulfing. The youth culture has been shaped by the engulfing medium of television.

As a result, radio itself had to change. Youth want to be engulfed by their media, and if radio was to continue a new dimension had to be added. It is significant that rock music appeared at just about the same time that television was becoming firmly established in homes. This provided radio with its needed new format. Rock music is engulfing. The sound is loud, intense and mixed together. The beat is more important than the words. There is no definite ending—the music just seems to fade out and another record starts to spin. Radio adapted itself to the impact of the new medium, the engulfing medium of television.

One does not have to agree with everything that McLuhan says to understand that television has been the most powerful force shaping the thought patterns and attitudes of our youth. Since we are now at the transition from stage two to stage three, the canyon between these two cultures may be greater than in the next generation.

But the canyon exists because of other factors as well. The adult portion of our society, those over 25, is almost outnumbered by those under 25. Because the youth generation is so large, we are far more aware of their problems. The problems separating the two cultures appear larger simply because the proportion of young people is so overwhelming.

Then you add the ingredient of rapid change. Life used to be simple for everyone. It was like simple farm life. But now even farming is a complex industry. Friedenberg[4] points out that every major industrial nation is faced with its own youth problem. As we move rapidly through the age of technology, the changes in urban life and growth in industry make life more complicated. And complications and change bring uncertainty. Margaret Mead points out that "the more intense the experience of generational change . . . the more brittle the social system becomes and the less secure the individual is likely to be."[5]

There is also rapid change in the amount of knowledge. Man's knowledge increased more in the last thirty years than in the previous two thousand. And the rate of increase is becoming even more rapid. As a result, the choice of a vocation is not only complicated by the vast number of possibilities, but also by the fear that the job may not even exist ten years from now! The adult generation feels these same pressures, but it is the youth generation, the youth culture, that is being formed and shaped by them.

SO WHAT?

Sounds like the generation gap is real, after all! Call it what you want. The important thing is that you recognize that the gap, or the canyon, is not a matter of *age* difference, but of different *cultures.* Francis Schaeffer, speaking to a group of ministers, referred to the existence of a generation gap, but then went on to define it in terms of a difference in cultures and attitudes.[6]

There is an important distinction to be made. As long as we think in terms of a gap between generations, how can it be bridged? The adult generation cannot get younger. But if we think of the gap as one between cultures, it can be bridged! In fact, the church has for centuries been bridging cultural canyons. In the church's activity in foreign missions, major cultures have been bridged and the message of Jesus Christ has been communicated. And since it is not a matter of age, but of cultures, age is not a factor. Some of the most effective youth counselors or youth Sunday school teachers are 40 plus. And they look like it. Nevertheless they have bridged the canyon between the two cultures.

How? The same way the effective missionary bridges the major cultural canyon between himself and the people in another country. He does not just sit at home reading about the other culture, although this kind of information is important. He does not get all upset about the differences between the two cultures, although he must be aware of them. And he cannot go with the intention of imposing *his* culture on another culture. None of these add up to building a bridge across cultures. Bridges are built as we get up, get involved with the people on the other side of the canyon, and start loving them as people. We can learn by reading about them, but real learning and understanding take place only as we enter into meaningful conversations with the members of the opposite culture. There is no substitute for getting involved and loving the people that make up the youth culture. And age need not be a barrier!

Some have suggested that the gap must be closed, the canyon must be covered over. This implies an unbalanced concern for the culture at the sacrifice of concern for the individuals in that culture. Our missions programs have made this mistake at times in the past. The objective of introducing people to Jesus Christ almost takes second place after the goal of changing the structures of a foreign culture. We can learn from their experience. Our objective in helping youth learn in our Sunday schools and church programs is not to change the youth culture, but to introduce individual members of that culture to the life-changing power of the Holy Spirit. Let us build bridges of communication and understanding as we seek to discover who is on the other side.

Somewhere deep
In disagreement
There is a link—a bond unbroken,
Of something shared and yet unspoken.
How can we reach that common spark
If neither youth nor age
Will cross the breach
And hear the truth
That lives in each?[7]

CHAPTER TWO

WHO IS ON THE OTHER SIDE?

Bridges *can* be built!

Adults and youth *can* communicate!

It is not an impossible situation. That is why we have coined a new phrase to describe the situation: culture canyon. Age is not the barrier to communication. Adults of all ages have found that time, patience and understanding are part of what it takes to bridge the canyon. But it takes even more. A person may have the time, but do nothing constructive with it. He may even have patience, but never put it to use. And understanding can be a mere word until *used* in a real situation. What else does it take? Three additional ingredients:

First, adults need to develop an awareness of what the youth culture is like. How do young people think? In what ways do they differ from the adult perspective? This involves an awareness of generalities, with the possibility of exceptions. But an understanding of the general viewpoints of the youth culture helps us develop tolerance of the differences. Part of this chapter will seek to present some of these differences.

Second, adults should have some knowledge of what the adolescent is like. How does the "typical" eighth grader act? How is the seventh grader different from the junior in high school? This is knowledge about the nature of the individual—an understanding to some degree of adolescent psychology. This will make up the other part of this chapter.

Third, adults must take time to sit down with individual members of the youth culture and get to know them as *people*. There is absolutely no substitute for stepping out and actually meeting members of the youth culture! You can read this book and every book in the bibliography, but the canyon will not be bridged until you actually get to know individual young people. This ingredient cannot be left out. You can become an expert on youth and their culture, but communication across the canyon only begins when adults start to meet them person-to-person.

Read on, but also get out of your chair and spend some time talking and *listening* to youth!

WHAT IS IT LIKE ON THE OTHER SIDE?

The electric age! So what? Has it really made a difference? What are the differences?

Through the medium of television, the world has shrunk. We are now quickly aware of the plights of our fellow men all over the globe. Our technological society is much more complex and the tensions and pressures are greater than ever. The tensions of the world belong to the individual because we are all part of a worldwide electronic communications network. And there are some important results in the life-perspective of youth today. We must be careful to remember that these are only generalizations. There are bound to be exceptions, but we can see certain general trends within the youth culture that set it apart from the adult culture. What is suggested here is by no means exhaustive, but does represent the major points of the differences.[1]

THEY HAVE LITTLE REVERENCE FOR WHAT THE OLDER GENERATION CONSIDERS SACRED

Youth today does not stand in awe of the sacred shrines of the past generations. Nothing is holy in the sense that they simply worship without understanding. If something is sacred, then there must be a valid reason why it is sacred.

Nationalism is an example. Many adults have the firm conviction that love for their country must be above question. They proudly attach the bumper sticker "My Country, Right or Wrong," or "America, Love It or Leave

It." Youth asks "Why?" From their perspective, God and country are not synonymous. So they reply with the bumper sticker, "America, Change It or Lose It." They are looking for meanings, not just blind acceptance.

Christianity comes under the same scrutiny. Young people shout, "Jesus—YES! Christianity—NO!" The church and Jesus Christ are not the same, at least not the churches they see. Jesus calls for action. His life was one of love and concern. The church seems interested only in forms and empty prayers. The needs of today cannot be met by yesterday's forms. These forms are sacred to adults, but youth today do not stand in awe.

In "Eleanor Rigby," the Beatles sing of Father McKenzie who writes a sermon that no one will hear—no one is listening. Later on as the lonely girl, Eleanor Rigby, dies, Father McKenzie conducts her funeral, which no one attends. As he walks from the grave, the words come, "no one was saved." Why? Concern about forms, about the style of the sermon, but little or no concern about obedience to the words of Christ to give a cup of water in His name.

Bob Dylan, Paul Simon and Janis Joplin are others who have put to music the question of what really is sacred in Christianity. Is it the forms of worship, or the teachings of Christ? Those of us who know the life-changing power of the gospel must confess that the life and death of Jesus Christ, along with the power of the Resurrection, form the heart of Christianity. Let's not get caught defending some comfortable form of worship or church government as being sacred and above question or change.

There is unfortunately another shrine which is rejected by the youth culture, and perhaps this rejection is most basic to the canyon separating the two groups. This is the shrine of *truth*.

Pilate asked the question, "What is truth?" and didn't wait for an answer. Today's youth do not even bother asking the question for they "know" that truth does not exist in any absolute form. The older generation was raised in an atmosphere that could say, "This is true!" But truth now is considered to be relative. Francis Schaeffer[2] traces this back to the philosopher Hegel, who said that you take a thesis—a statement. You then take an antithesis—which is its opposite. What results is a synthesis, or a blending of the two ideas. Young people have been taught to think in this manner. Adults think in a logical pattern in which the effect follows the cause and an opposite cause makes an opposite effect.

The adult perspective says that "truth does not equal nontruth." But the new approach says that you add what is supposed to be truth to its opposite and the result is "new-truth" which is also added to its opposite, and so on.

This can be illustrated like this:

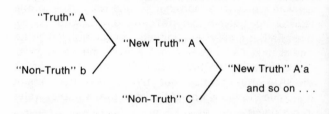

McLuhan speaks of this same thing when he points out that the adult generation is used to thinking in a linear pattern of cause and effect. The thought pattern of youth is multidirectional.[3]

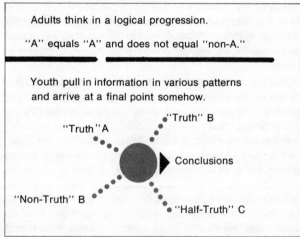

A person feeds a number of theses and antitheses into his thinking and experiences synthesis—"truth." What one experiences may be completely different from what another experiences, but both can be "true," say the young, because there is no objective, absolute truth. Thus the young measure truth against their own experience.

You may agree with some of the irreverence of the young towards nationalism and "Churchianity," but we must resist any dilution of the truth of God's saving activity in Jesus Christ. We cannot measure the truth of the Bible and the claims of Christ against our experience. Bridging the canyon does not mean adopting the thought patterns of the youth culture. It does mean that we seek to understand how they think, and then use this understanding in our approach with them.

THEY ARE HUMANISTIC

This means simply that they are concerned about being human. They are interested in the meaning of being a person. The key word seems to be *meaningfulness*. How can I be a complete person in such a messed up world? How can I help my brother be a more complete person? These are some of the questions young people are asking. They are good questions, and loaded with implications for adults.

One result of this humanism is a rejection of the old Puritan work ethic. For the young, work must have meaning and must bring satisfaction. Life is more than just a job. As a result, the Peace Corps, VISTA, and similar programs attract increasing numbers of volunteers. The social sciences, particularly the areas such as social work, sociology, and psychology attract the interest of youth. They are still seeking an answer to Solomon's question in Ecclesiastes 1:3: *What does man gain from all his labour and his toil here under the sun?*[4] Young people find satisfaction as they give themselves in service to help their fellow man.

Their humanistic concern also leads them to seek a greater depth of meaning in their relationships with their friends. They look at the adult culture, and with Paul Simon they see people going through the motions of talking, listening and trying to say something, but no one really says anything or hears anything. The "Sounds of Silence" are the sounds of an empty and meaningless generation. They form empty relationships with no concern about getting involved in helping others live.

Paul Simon later described a positive concern for others in his song, "Bridge Over Troubled Water" where he speaks of the kind of relationship that will continue even when troubles are deep and intense.

The Christian church hears these words and says that Jesus is the bridge over troubled water. And He is! But the point of the song is that *we* are to be a bridge for our friend as he goes through troubled water. Jesus is the bridge over the troubled water of sin. But our living faith calls us to bear one another's burdens—to mourn with the mourners (Galatians 6:2; Romans 12:15). We are called to a concern about the joys and sorrows of our fellow man.

THEY LOVE THE SPONTANEOUS EXPRESSIONS OF LIFE

For an experience to be full of meaning, young people feel it should be spontaneous. There should be freedom of expression. All the senses cry out for involvement, for an experience of the joys and sufferings of life.

Television bombards young people with life and they want to respond. Some demonstrate and riot as a means of expressing their empathy and response to certain events. Others quietly volunteer and sacrificially give themselves, working to change a little bit of the world. To "do their own thing" is youth's attempt to be spontaneous in their response to life.

Spontaneous rap sessions are also an important element of the youth culture. Time fades in importance as the discussion grows and deepens in intensity. These events are what life is all about. This is where learning takes place.

Some of the old forms of Christian expression are adopted by the Christian youth culture. "Jesus Saves" buttons, fearless witnessing, and testimony meetings become spontaneous expressions of their faith in Christ.

A church near San Francisco has seen their Sunday

evening service grow from about 250 to over 1,100 in less than a year. Why? An explanation almost sounds corny. But when you visit, you witness spontaneous events which are a genuine expression of faith in Christ. People give testimonies of both joy and problems. When someone shares a problem, such as needing a job, prayer is part of the response, but someone is also assigned to help that person find a job the next day. The offering is a "give and take" offering—give if God has blessed you; take if you have a need. (The taking is limited to under $10. If a person needs more than that, he can speak to one of the ministers after the service.) There's a good variety of music and solid teaching of the Scriptures. You will also find a concern for meaning rather than form, and a genuine concern for the total needs of a man, both physical *and* spiritual. These elements, added together, account for the growth and the high percentage of young people (over half are under 25).

THEY QUESTION AND REJECT THE STRUCTURES WHICH TEND TO MANIPULATE PEOPLE

This is almost a natural outgrowth of the first three points. Any structure (whether in society, business, government or the church) which tends to manipulate people is certainly more concerned with form than with meaning, is certainly unspontaneous and rigid and has little concern for man as a person.

War is rejected as the ultimate form of dehumanizing and manipulation. Some young people drop out of society as their way of rejecting war. Others contradict themselves as they violently protest against the violence of war. Still others speak with deep concern, making their points again through bumper stickers, such as the ironic "War is good business, invest your son."

They enter the business world and find that they must become part of the corporate image. Some adjust, others resist and drop out.

Even the church appears to be in the business of maintaining the church as an institution. The church falls into the same trap of fitting people into the harness so they can "function" and the system can continue. Little concern about *being,* only about keeping things going.

Young people feel that structures should facilitate the spontaneous expression of life and meaning. Anything else tends to manipulate. Structures in society in general, or in the church specifically, should be there for a reason: to keep people from interfering with each other, to facilitate growth, to help people in the church, to minister to each other. These kinds of structures are sought, others are rejected.

Who can argue with these points? It is difficult to study them and not identify with most of them, or at least with the spirit they represent. And it is a spirit of hope!

To defend the form for form's sake is to be a modern Pharisee. Jesus was concerned about the heart of man and His sharpest rebukes were directed against the Pharisees and their concern for ritual and form. Today's youth cry out against the adult culture and the concern for form instead of meaning. They are seeking to make the sacred things of the past meaningful for today.

Young people's search for the meaning of personhood has led them to the person of Jesus Christ. Even hippies "groove" on Jesus. We have preached that meaning in life is found in Jesus Christ. Young people are looking for meaning, and if they see it genuinely demonstrated in a person's life, they will recognize it.

An adult is on his way to bridging the culture canyon when he can appreciate and in some measure understand the young person's point of view. He does not have to agree with them. He does have to be real—and willing to grapple with the issues that concern youth. He should at least be able to understand the point they are trying to make, and why they feel so strongly about it.

In the process of wrestling with issues, whether in the Sunday school class or in an informal discussion, the adult's experience and life must be linked closely with the content of what he teaches and says. Note that the word is *linked.* He does not have to limit what he teaches and says to what he has experienced. But he must be in the process of experiencing, and open enough to relate where he is in that process. He must be growing, and as he grows he must be honest enough to share what is happening within his life.

Some of youth's concerns are not really new. Each generation has had to face these issues to some degree. But there is a new intensity of concern. What we are seeing is an *implosion*—an inward-directed explosion. Technology, along with our ability to be involved in events around the world as they happen, has helped to create this new intensity.

As a result, not everyone on the youthful side of the canyon is under 25. Many older adults have been caught up in the spirit of the new perspective. Conversely, many of the young have resisted the influence of the youth culture. As a result, there are youth who think like the older generation and adults who think like young people. This is why we call it a culture canyon instead of a generation gap.

But remember, we are not talking about these exceptions. We are describing the perspective of most members of the young generation, the youth culture. And an understanding of their perspective helps us begin to build bridges of communication.

SO WHO IS ON THE OTHER SIDE?

Since we are speaking about the majority of the members of the youth culture, it is safe to say that those on the other side are mostly adolescents. Intense, looking for meaning, spontaneous, and living in the now—but still adolescents.

Today's youth culture has its special marks; the faddish styles in clothes, the length of the hair, and the beat of the transistor radios. All of these are part of the embellishments of the youth culture. But when you sit down with one member of the youth culture, and get to know him, you find a person who is still concerned basically with the problems of being a teen-ager.

The word *adolescent* comes from a latin term, *adolescere,* which means "to grow, to grow to maturity." Apparently it has always been a troublesome period in man's growth. Shakespeare, in "A Winter's Tale" wrote,

"I would there were no age
between ten an' three and twenty,
or that youth would sleep out the rest."
But these years do exist, and they do have their peculiar problems and needs.

Erik Erikson has called this stage in man's growth the age of Identity Crisis. The goal of the adolescent is to find an identity.[5] He wants an answer to the question, "Who am I?" Related to this search for identity is the problem of self-acceptance and acceptance by his peers. Merton Strommen, in his study on youth,[6] found that two out of three young people interviewed had problems on this point. And at least 25% of them had *serious* problems in this area. The junior high youth is particularly bothered on this point. He is changing so quickly that he has a hard time just keeping up with what is happening to him. He needs to be aware of the fact that this is a time of change, so that self-acceptance at this stage is acceptance of change.

In Strommen's study, adults were also questioned. They considered the area of family relations as the most troubling area. Youth ranked this area as the least troubling area. That sharp difference points up another important need—understanding. Young people want to be understood by their parents. Real communication across the canyon will bring understanding, and this will help give young people a sense of worthiness and of meaning. This goes a long way in helping them accept themselves as they are.

These are also difficult years because of the shift from dependence to independence. Adolescence is a time of *preparation* for independence, not of actual independence. The young person is eager to be free, but still is not quite ready to accept all the responsibility that independence requires. The junior high youth is tossed about by this conflict. One moment he is asserting his independence, the next moment he seeks the reassurance that he can still depend on Mom and Dad. These fluctuations will tend to lessen as adults give youth opportunities for responsibility and as they move on through senior high school.

Doubts are distressing to any age group. But young

people feel a certain loneliness in their doubts. They need to see that doubts are a sign of growth. Doubts show that they are thinking about their faith. But they need help. Adult workers with youth who are open about their own questions will find a warm response. Young people seem to be aware of their needs. They sincerely want help from adults who are willing to set aside the "pat answers" and face the real issues.

HOW DOES HE DEVELOP?

What can the adult expect from a young person at any given age? How does the junior high differ from the senior high? What can one expect from a class of eighth graders? Or twelfth graders?

There are problems in any attempt to answer these questions. We are forced to deal with the hypothetical "average adolescent." Thus we cannot avoid generalizing. An actual teen-ager may not be exactly like the description in this book. You may find that this year's class of ninth graders has characteristics different from last year's class of ninth graders. The observant teacher or leader will not make hasty assumptions. He will spend time getting acquainted with his young people and learning what they are really like.

For our purposes, adolescence begins with junior high, or seventh grade. Suddenly elementary school and childhood are left behind. The twelve-year-old enters the world of youth! He is eager to become a part of this new world. There is an enthusiasm and an *outward* direction in his activity. He wants to be a part of the crowd. No longer is he content with just one friend. Now it must be plural—friends.

He also starts to think differently. Whereas the facts of the story satisfied him before, now he wants to know *why*. He starts to think abstractly. Principles begin to take on a new meaning, for he is able to understand them as a form of thought. He begins to test the facts he has previously accepted. He may experience questions and doubts. But these elements are just emerging; traces of childhood still linger.

Then comes eighth grade, and the outgoing enthusiasm turns *inward*. He is no longer so eager, for he is not entirely sure of himself. The girls grow at a rapid rate during this year. So the thirteen-year-old is cautious. It almost seems as though he goes into a period of hibernation until he feels he can cope with himself and also with other people. His rate of growth leads to an increase in insecurity and concern over acceptance.

Mentally, he becomes very *reflective*. As he turns inward, due to the physical changes he is undergoing, he also starts working through some of the new insights he is able to grasp. As he works through these ideas, he is on his way to developing a perspective on life. His peers continue to exert great influence, as do older youth. This is a time of mimicking. The eighth grader looks for leaders to follow and to imitate. This is all part of his search for his own identity.

Suddenly, he is in the ninth grade, and what a difference! He is almost grown up. Once again he moves *outward*. He has a new eagerness to express himself. He is more secure and so he can open up again to the outside world. Girls begin to develop womanly proportions, and the guys start to notice. It is usually a *happy* time, for he is starting to find out how to communicate his feelings.

With his growth comes problems. The ninth grader is far removed from the world of the seventh grader. There is also a sharp distinction between the ninth grader and those in the eighth grade. Yet many churches keep them in the same department at Sunday school. They often attend the same junior high schools. The differences raise some problems in organizing a youth department to best meet the needs of seventh, eighth, and ninth graders. This will be discussed further in chapter five.

Gesell and Ilg note that the tenth grade is often called the "fifteen-year-old-slump."[7] Again the adolescent turns *inward*. He seems so overwhelmed by the changes taking place within that he simply retreats inside his shell and attempts to sort things out. This gives him an air of indifference. He is unsure of himself, and finds it much safer to pull in and shut off the rest of the world.

The adult can be of most help at this age by simply being available, when needed, and serving as a sounding board to the young person's questions and ideas. It is a time of ups and downs as well as a time of changing interests. What holds his attention today will bore him tomorrow. So the understanding ear of the adult will listen with patience and understanding. Conversely, the prying adult will only shut off communication and widen the canyon.

In fact, the canyon is probably at its widest point at age fifteen. If we were in an airplane looking down on the hypothetical canyon separating the two cultures, it might look something like this:

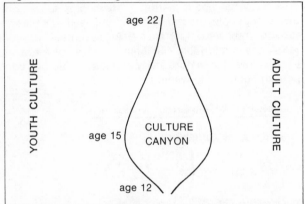

The rift begins to widen around age twelve. From this point it grows rapidly to its largest gap at age fifteen. Gesell and Ilg stress the point that the fifteen-year-old is not just an older fourteen-year-old. He is more a pre-sixteen-year-old. He does not look back, except to pull things together for the big push towards adulthood.

Beginning at age sixteen, the canyon starts to close until around age 22, when the former adolescent is a part of the adult world. Sixteen marks his entrance into the preadult stage. He is becoming *self-reliant* as he feels that he has passed the major part of the journey through adolescence. Even the adults treat him as though he were almost one of them.

Along with this comes a feeling of independence. He is not fighting for independence anymore—he is using it. This gives him a growing feeling of self-assurance as he is finding himself as a person and starting to like what he finds. Since he feels more comfortable with himself, he is able to develop a new quality in his relationship with the opposite sex. He develops meaningful friendships, although the girls take them more seriously than the guys do. He has his problems, but generally age sixteen is still "sweet sixteen."

From seventeen onward, the road smooths out. The teen-ager realizes that he is on the threshold of adulthood—that childhood and adolescence are almost things of the past. This realization points him toward decisions concerning the future. What next? Vocation now or college? What about marriage? He begins to become aware of people and issues beyond himself. His parents take on a renewed importance as the seventeen-year-old feels more comfortable with them. He develops the ability to be involved in mature study and leadership positions both in society and within the church.

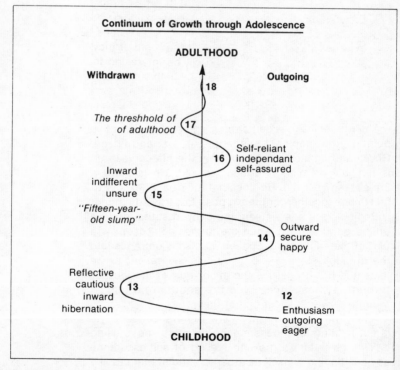

Continuum of Growth through Adolescence

ADULTHOOD

Withdrawn   Outgoing

18

*The threshhold of
of adulthood* 17

16 Self-reliant
independant
self-assured

Inward
indifferent
unsure 15

*"Fifteen-year-
old slump"*

14 Outward
secure
happy

Reflective
cautious 13
inward
hibernation

12
Enthusiasm
outgoing
eager

CHILDHOOD

Again, these are generalizations. There will be exceptions. In fact, one whole group at a particular age level can be an exception. A ninth grade class may be quiet and withdrawn, like the eighth graders are supposed to be. It might be good to illustrate this as a progression of growth and maturity.

Since growth is a progression, we resist the tendency to put our ninth graders in the "ninth-grade-box." Instead, we try to find out why they are at a different point in the growth pattern than expected. Perhaps they are at a tenth grade level—the fifteen-year-old-slump. This might be due to the presence of several strong leaders among the class who have pushed the others in their development. Or they might be at the eighth grade level due to the lack of any strong leaders in the group.

Adults learn about teens by observation—listening to their discussions, talking with them, reading their written work. We find out whether they are at the eighth grade or tenth grade level by observing their relationships with and attitudes toward the opposite sex. If they are behind, the sexes will sit on opposite sides of the room. If they are ahead of schedule, the boys will be interested in the girls. The adult will also observe whether they are lingering in childhood in the way they think and act, as the eighth grader does, or straining toward the goal of adulthood, as the tenth grader will be starting to do.

One teacher might spend an entire year working with a class, helping them mature to a certain level of development. Then promotion comes and he finds his new students are so advanced that they start in where the previous class left off. If our diagram were a rigid system, he might wonder if anything was accomplished during his year with the first class. But with the progression he simply sees the new class as starting at a higher level of maturity than the previous class. His goal, then, is to help them move ahead.

Yes, the canyon can be bridged! We build different bridges with each age level, but we can build bridges. What then? Adults and young people learn and grow together toward the common goal of maturity in Jesus Christ.

FOOTNOTES

CHAPTER 1

1 · Ross Snyder, *Youth and Their Culture* (Nashville: Abingdon, 1969), p. 24.
2 · Marshall McLuhan, *Understanding Media: The Extensions of Man* (New York: McGraw-Hill Book Co., 1964), p. ix. Marshall McLuhan, Director of the Center for Culture and Technology at the University of Toronto, is recognized as one of the most creative and influential men in the field of communications and media.
3 · Will Durant, *The Reformation* (New York: Simon and Schuster, 1957), p. 160.
4 · Edgar Z. Friedenberg, *Coming of Age in America* (New York: Random House, 1963), p. 3.
5 · Margaret Mead, *Culture and Commitment* (New York: Doubleday, 1970), p. 59.
6 · Dr. Francis A. Schaeffer, at the "Youth, the Church, and the World" Conference held at Buck Hill Falls, Pennsylvania, March, 1970. Francis A. Schaeffer is the director of L'Abri Fellowship in Switzerland, where thousands of young people have found a home and new meaning in life through Jesus Christ.
7 · Phyllis Reynolds Naylor, *Ships in the Night* (Philadelphia: Fortress Press, 1971).

CHAPTER 2

1 · Dennis Benson, *The Now Generation* (Richmond: John Knox Press, 1969).
2 · Francis A. Schaeffer, *The God Who Is There* (Downers Grove, Ill.: Inter-Varsity Press, 1968), pp. 20 ff.
3 · McLuhan, *Understanding Media,* pp. 292, 293.
4 · Ecclesiastes 1:3, From *The New English Bible.* © The Delegates of the Oxford University Press and the Syndics of the Cambridge University Press 1961, 1970. Reprinted by permission.
5 · Erik H. Erikson, *Youth Identity and Crisis* (New York: W.W. Norton and Co., 1968), p. 17.
6 · Merton P. Strommen, *Profiles of Church Youth* (St. Louis: Concordia Publishing House, 1963), pp. 89 ff.
7 · Arnold Gesell, Frances L. Ilg, and Louise Bates Ames, *Youth, the Years from Ten to Sixteen* (New York: Harper and Brothers, 1964), p. 219.

PART II

YOUTH—THE WAY THEY LEARN

CHAPTER THREE

LEARNING MORE ABOUT LEARNING

It was a first-time experience for most of them. Several had wanted to try skiing but had never had the courage to do it by themselves. Now they stood as a group looking up at the sweeping grandeur of the snow-covered mountains. It was still early, so not many skiers were on the slopes yet. But those who were there glided gracefully down the hill making it look quite easy.

"Nothing to it," exclaimed Greg, as he watched; "Let me at it." The response of the other teen-agers was a few raised eyebrows and a nervous laugh or two.

It took time to rent skis, boots and poles, but finally Greg was ready to give it a try. He stood there a minute looking first at the rope tow and then at the beginners' slope. "Let's go!" he said to the group's advisor.

"Wait until I can show you how to stop, Greg."

"That's easy. I'm going up," replied Greg. He grabbed the rope tow and was on his way.

After reaching the top, Greg took a deep breath, shuffled his skis back and forth a couple of times, and with a "Here goes nothing!" he pushed off. Everything was okay for the first hundred yards or so, but then he noticed he was going faster than he wanted. He also realized he was going across as well as down, and was heading for the trees.

Two automatic reactions set in: Everybody heard a loud *Aaaaaaaaaaugh,* as Greg leaned into the hill to try to make his skis turn uphill and stop. The loud cry was climaxed by a *thud.* Everyone laughed except Greg as he sat there checking all his bones.

About five hours later, the advisor's wife, who had

come up late, stood with her husband watching the members of the group skiing down the hill in various stages of proficiency. She watched Greg making some graceful moves through the mounds of snow and asked, "How did he learn to ski like that?"

"It wasn't easy," was all her husband could reply.

WHAT IS LEARNING?

How does a person learn to ski? At what point in those five hours did Greg learn to ski? How does a person learn to drive or to multiply or to share his faith with a friend? By looking at what happened to Greg in those five hours, can we find out how a person learns? Are there some basic principles?

LEARNING IS A PROCESS

There was no single run down the slope that turned Greg from a nonskier into a skier. It was not a single event, but a *process.*

On another level, at what point does a first-grade child "learn" that two-plus-two equals four? Is it when the teacher tells him that truth? When she shows him with blocks? When he correctly places four blocks into a box, two at a time? When he can say, "Two plus two equals four"? Or when he answers the question correctly on his first arithmetic test? Can you pick the point at which the first-grader "learned"? Just as Greg learned to ski through a process, the first grader's learning was a series of events—a process.

Learning is a personal process. It is the learner who learns. That may sound obvious, but there are teachers who teach as though learning were the automatic result of telling. Telling does not equal learning. Few people, after hearing a lecture on skiing, would venture to the top of the slope the first time they put on skis. Greg may have studied skiing methods, but learning did not take place until Greg got out on the slope and tried to ski.

When it comes to learning the truths of Scripture, many teachers forget that learning is what the learner does, not what the teacher does. Perhaps this is because we tend to confuse the authority of the Scripture with the "authority" of the teacher of Scripture. The two are not synonymous. In teaching the Bible, we start with the authority of the Scripture. It is authoritative in and of itself. The teacher can confidently say, "This is what the Bible says; read it for yourself and judge your behavior in its light."

The problem is not that we need to be convinced of this authority, but that we do not allow the learner to search out this authority and make it his own. We are too eager to give him the answer instead of the means to finding the answer.

For example, Mike sits quietly in class each Sunday and listens carefully to the discussion. The teacher knows from conversation with him that Mike is grasping the ideas being discussed. He is finally motivated to ask a question in the class. Based on his own experience, and on what he has heard in the discussions, he does not agree with a certain conclusion. So he challenges the teacher. How does the teacher answer? Does he help Mike explore the Scripture to find his answer there, or is the teacher afraid that Mike might come up with the "wrong" answer?

If the teacher gives Mike the "right answer," he is relying on the authority of the teacher rather than on the authority of the Scriptures. And he is forgetting that learning is a *personal* process—something that Mike must be involved in personally. By simply telling Mike the answer, the teacher has dealt with his question, but he has not allowed Mike to learn the answer for himself. To return to the illustration of skiing, the sponsor may have told Greg how to do a snowplow turn, but Greg did not really learn how until he could experiment with what he had been told and prove it for himself.

Learning is also a *social* process. This is not a contradiction of the personal nature of learning. One might say that learning is a personal process that generally takes place in a social context.

Marshall McLuhan said, "The medium is the message."[1] This is like the old saying, "What you are speaks so loudly that I can't hear what you say." Young people learn not just from teachers, but from each other. When they come to Sunday school, they learn more from the way the teacher presents the lesson material, how he reacts to the members of the group, and how the group members react to each other, than from the actual words of the lesson. The teacher's preparation and the appearance of the room often drown out the teacher's words. The process of learning takes place in a social context.

Too often, training within the church has emphasized the individualistic nature of learning, while neglecting the dynamics of the group. Even when group methods are used, they are generally used to get individuals involved, not to take advantage of group dynamics in learning. Part III of this book will deal with this matter.

LEARNING IS CHANGE

Since learning is a process, it follows that learning is also change. A process involves change. Greg changed from a nonskier to a skier. This was a change in his action. Martha Leypoldt points out that change can also take place in the area of feeling and knowing.[2] A person's understanding, his attitudes, or his actions are changed when he learns.

Change also involves direction. A person can be changed toward the right goals or the wrong goals. In fact, it could be said that in just about every situation learning is taking place. If the room is messy, hot and crowded, and the teacher is dull, students are learning that this activity is really not that important. They are learning to turn off what is happening around them. If the teacher is constantly drilling the class for "right" answers, students can learn to listen enough to keep him off their back. But they are not learning anything positive. They are only learning how to get through an uncomfortable situation. This is change in the wrong direction.

In the experimental stage of using the total hour concept (described in chapter 5 of this book), one junior high department found changes in attitudes happening simply as a result of the new approach. One girl who had been a particular problem in the church program as well as at home got excited about what was happening. Previously she did everything to stay home on Sunday mornings. But about the fourth week of the program, she came stamping up to the youth director and said, "I'm mad!" He thought to himself, "So what else is new, you're always mad." He simply said "So?" out loud. She repeated and explained: "I'm mad! Our group was all ready to do our roleplay and the bell rang. We didn't get our chance. I can't wait until next week!" With that she turned and walked away, leaving the youth director with his chin on the ground in amazement.

What happened? She was starting to learn. And as a result there were some changes in her attitudes. Since then she has changed some of her actions as well. Learning is change.

Looking for changes in our students will serve as a good measure of how much learning is taking place. As we examine what is causing the changes in our students, we will become aware of how we can lead people in the process of learning. We will become confirmed optimists about the joys of learning. We will see that the biggest problems in a class cry out for change through learning. And learning is what we are here to provide.

LEARNING IS ECSTASY

Are you getting excited about the possibilities? Good! For excitement and ecstasy are parts of learning also. Imagine Greg, back on the ski slopes. He is in the process of learning as he is being changed from a nonskier to a skier. And gradually it seems to be getting easier. The skis are staying together. The spills happen less frequently, the turns are not quite as panic filled. And on one of those runs down the hill, it's fun! Greg gets excited—wow! What a thrill! **Ecstasy!**[3]

Or think back to that first grader. He listens intently as the teacher explains the equation. He watches as she demonstrates how the addition of two blocks to two blocks equals four blocks. The teacher poses the question: "Two plus two equals what?" Our first grader thinks a moment. Then his eyes get wider and his hand shoots into the air as he shouts out with *joy,* "I know, I know!" **Ecstasy!**

How long has it been since your class has experienced the joy of learning? Not necessarily fun, but joy. Ecstasy does not do away with the disciplines of learning. On the contrary, discipline gives meaning to ecstasy. Look at the musician, or the artist. He has had to master the techniques of his art in order that he can enjoy the ecstasy of achievement. "The process of mastery itself can be ecstatic, leading to delight that transcends mastery."[4] The thrill of skiing under control. The ecstasy of mastering a multiplication table. The joy of discovering the application of a new truth from God's Word. These are part of the process of learning.

NOW THE PROCESS OF LEARNING PROGRESSES

We have seen that learning is a process that produces change in a person's attitudes, understanding and actions. But change can be either positive or negative. If it is moving in a positive direction, we can call it "growth." In the context of the teaching and learning experiences of the Sunday school change can mean growth *in grace, and in the knowledge of our Lord and Saviour Jesus Christ.*[5]

The progress of our growth can be stated as occurring on four levels or stages. The first is **familiarization.** This is really the level of preparation for learning. In this stage, the teacher gives the information, either as an introduction or as an overview of the materials. This is the information needed to get the learner started. The student is involved mentally as he listens to the information. To introduce the quarter's study on the book of Acts to the eighth graders, a departmental leader presented in the first session some background information on the setting for the first church. He talked about the fears of the disciples, the power of the Roman government and the hostility of the Jews toward Jesus' followers. He used a lecture method, for his purpose was to convey information. He also could have used a research and report method with the students receiving advance assignments and presenting reports. In any case, the material would have had a discourse-type presentation with learners participating passively. The purpose is to give information—facts—with the meaning coming later.

Another approach might be to present an overview of the material for the unit, raising some questions that will be answered during the unit.

Unfortunately, many teachers never go beyond this level of learning. Their sole purpose in teaching is to convey information and the lecture method is their method of presentation. There is a place for the lecture. It *is* the first stage in the learning process. But the teacher who remains at this level constantly runs the risk that the learner will soon forget the information. The learner may not find the material relevant for his life. He is relatively passive, and apart from the working of the Holy Spirit, learning is left to chance.

The lecture is still an important stage in the learning process. Used skillfully for the purpose of familiarization, it will accomplish its objective in the stages of learning.

Once we have conveyed the necessary information, learning moves into the second stage, **feedback.** This can be defined as any response from the learner "fed back" to the learning leader. The student is now involved verbally. In the illustration of Mike used earlier in this chapter, his challenge to the teacher was feedback. He was responding to the information presented. Sometimes a learner's response may be negative, such as a bored yawn or the failure to return to class next week. These are negative means through which the learner lets the teacher know that he is not coming through.

From the positive perspective, feedback is the beginning of the student's involvement in the learning process. The student is beginning to work with the facts that have been presented. He is beginning to inquire as to the meaning of the material.

Some teachers are threatened by this inquiring and searching. To such a teacher a question is a personal challenge, especially if he thinks of himself as the authority figure in the class. A question is a challenge to that authority. In most cases, however, the question means that the learner is beginning to use his reasoning powers and is attempting to come to grips with the material being presented.

The relaxed and confident teacher will respond to questions with some questions of his own, aimed at motivating the learner to continue in the process of learning. This presupposes that the familiarization stage was adequate so that the learner has some basic facts at hand to use in the process.

In order to encourage feedback, the class will be semistructured with some of the following characteristics:

There will be freedom to explore ideas in dialogue with the others in the class as well as with the teacher. Alternatives will be explored in the light of the Scriptures. The learner will have been involved in the first stage and will be familiar with the basics of the material. He will then have the understanding necessary for asking intelligent questions and arriving at some tentative conclusions on his own.

There will be a concern to find the meaning of the material and how it applies to the individuals and to the group. The relevance of different ideas will be questionedand explored. The learner will be free to make mistakes as he asks questions and explores ideas.

Basically, this feedback stage is one of questioning and inquiry as students and teacher raise questions to test the materials being presented. Discussions, question and answer, and brainstorming are some of the methods used at this level in the process of learning.

Following feedback is the third stage of learning, the level of **exploration.** The most obvious difference between this level and the feedback level is location. Feedback is usually done in the context of the classroom. Exploration moves out of the classroom and occurs in many places. There is still the characteristic of testing information, but now the learner is given more responsibility in limited areas of study. He is involved personally. The teacher is still available for consultation and advice when problems arise.

Exploration may develop as a question is raised during the feedback stage. As discussion continues on the question it becomes obvious that more information is necessary, so the wise teacher will make some assignments for research and reporting back to the group.

Or the teacher may see that opinions are varied in spite of what seems to be clear in the Scriptures. He will divide the class into small study groups and give an assignment to each group. After a certain amount of time, in which the students are involved in study independent from the teacher, the group is called back together and insights are shared with the whole class.

Exploration involves a certain risk. Students may be inadequately prepared for this stage of learning. This would lead to a pooling of ignorance rather than a sharing of insight. Time may be used inefficiently as students move from small group to large group. Research groups may fail to do any research, reporting back empty-handed and empty-headed. These problems can be minimized by careful delegation, with some checking up done by the teacher.

The advantages of exploration are many. Since learning is a changing process marked by joyful discovery, the extension of the classroom to include the world increases the opportunities. Projects done during the week extend the class time throughout the week. A student's sense of responsibility increases as he sees what he can do when given an assignment. The joy of success fosters self-respect, which in turn encourages openness on the part of both student and teacher. Self-respect also reinforces the process begun at level two—feedback—where the student gets actively involved in the process of learning. He is also working with facts to discover their meanings in relation to the experiences of life.

The final stage is really the objective of the whole process of learning: **responsibility.**⁶ At this level, the learner is responsible for his own continued learning and growth. He is probably able to take on more responsibility as well, perhaps as a learning leader.

Obviously, the learner's age has something to do with this level. The seventh grader will be less likely to achieve this level than the high school senior. Nevertheless, it is still the teacher's objective even in the seventh grade class. And the way he guides the seventh grader will affect that student's ability to progress and grow and become a responsible learner in the twelfth grade.

One church has been very effective in accomplishing this aim. Instead of using adult teachers in their twelfth grade department, they have chosen "student learning leaders." These are high school seniors who meet on Wednesday evening to discuss the Sunday morning material; on Sunday morning, they lead the small group study sessions. This is *responsible* learning! And this was Paul's admonition when he wrote, *Let the word of Christ dwell in you richly, as you teach and admonish one another in all wisdom.*[7]

Adults need to be creative, willing to give young people the responsibility for learning. The exploration stage becomes a testing ground to find out who is both willing and able to move on to the level of responsibility. Those who are ready are given opportunity to learn at that level.

It might help at this point to visualize these stages in the learning process.

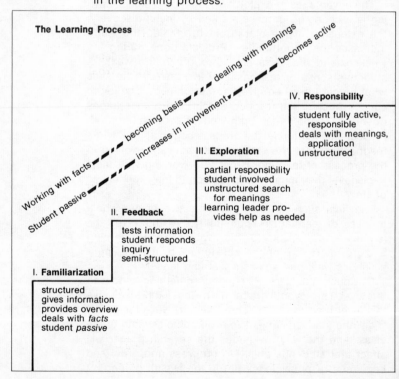

The Learning Process

Working with facts ▬▬ *Student passive* ▬▬ *becoming basis* ▬▬ *increases in involvement* ▬▬ *dealing with meanings* ▬▬ *becomes active*

IV. Responsibility
student fully active,
responsible
deals with meanings,
application
unstructured

III. Exploration
partial responsibility
student involved
unstructured search
  for meanings
learning leader pro-
  vides help as needed

II. Feedback
tests information
student responds
inquiry
semi-structured

I. Familiarization
structured
gives information
provides overview
deals with *facts*
student *passive*

The student is less involved—relatively passive—at the familiarization level. His involvement is mental. As he continues on into the feedback stage and into the exploration stage, his level of active involvement increases. When he reaches the responsibility stage, he is totally involved, totally active in the process of learning. There is a continuum from mental involvement to active, responsible involvement.

There is another simultaneous progression involved in the learning process: the student moves from bare facts to meaningful application of the facts. In familiarization, we are limited to the facts, perhaps with hints at their application and importance. The feedback stage involves the questioning of these facts in an attempt to integrate them into our lives. And as we move through exploration and responsibility, the application of the meaning behind the facts becomes a necessary ingredient.

There is much more that could be said about learning. First of all, keep learning yourself! All too often, the young person graduates from high school or college, and with a sigh of relief vows never to study again. What a loss! The adult working with youth needs to set the example by being a growing person, constantly learning and looking for new and better ways to involve other people in learning. This is part of the role of being a "learning leader."

THE HOLY SPIRIT AND THE LEARNING PROCESS

We have been looking at the natural growth process of the individual as he continues to learn. The primary Motivator and Guide in learning about the Scriptures is the Holy Spirit. Two basic assumptions undergird the learning experience of the Sunday school: that the Scriptures form the heart and foundation of what we teach; and that the teacher has discovered for himself a living faith in the Christ who is central to those Scriptures. But a class can have these two ingredients and still fall short of exciting learning. It takes the Holy Spirit to activate the learning situation. Roy Zuck points out that "the Holy Spirit, working through the Word of God, is the spiritual dynamic for Christian living."[8] When we see Christian education, Christian learning, as change in the way persons live before God, we recognize that we must have the work and ministry of the Holy Spirit present both in the teacher and in the learner.

THE WORK OF THE HOLY SPIRIT AS MOTIVATOR

Motivation is one of the key problems in education. Paul gives the key to motivation: *It is God who is at work within you, giving you the will and the power to achieve his purpose.*[9] And God's purpose is that we might *grow up in every way into Christ.*[10] The Holy Spirit provides the inner motivation to learn. The Holy Spirit works with the learner's inner drives and desires, directing him to want to learn and grow. He does this by making us aware of our needs. He creates the hunger, the sense of weakness that is necessary sometimes to get us going, to get us motivated.

Donald Joy points out that meaningful learning takes place best when content collides with our needs.[11] This will almost automatically set in motion the learning process. For example, during the week Eric was told off by one of his friends. Eric was talking to this friend about his faith: he had just shared how he felt that Jesus Christ was the only way to get to God, and that only those accepting Christ as Lord and Saviour could share in salvation. The friend called Eric a narrow-minded bigot and walked away. Eric's problem was not just the insult his former friend hurled at him; it was complicated by doubts within his own mind about the exclusive nature of Christian faith. During the rest of the week, the struggle intensified.

Sunday morning came and Eric was in his class. He was not very involved in what was taking place until he heard the teacher introduce the new unit of study: "Understanding Other Faiths." Eric perked up a bit, just in time to hear the teacher say that the gospel of Jesus Christ is unique and exclusive. Suddenly Eric heard himself toss the question to the teacher, "Why is it the only way?"

"Glad you asked that, Eric," the reply came back, "Because that was my next question—Why? Let's divide into groups of three or four. I'll give each group a different passage of Scripture and we'll see what the Word of God has to say about the exclusive nature of our salvation."

Suddenly Eric is motivated to learn. The content of the material had a head-on collision with his own needs. The Holy Spirit was at work in Eric, stirring up the questions in his mind and motivating him in the process of learning.

Sometimes a teacher who discourages the students from asking questions can block the Holy Spirit's work of motivating. Lack of motivation can also be traced to a poor room environment, or to a teacher's lack of concern for making practical applications from the material. Teachers need to be careful not to "quench the Spirit" and His working within the class session. Seeking to lead students to the level of **responsibility** in the learning process will provide the context in which the Holy Spirit is free to motivate.

THE WORK OF THE HOLY SPIRIT AS ENLIGHTENER

Not only does the Holy Spirit motivate students to learn, He also gives them the ability to do so by providing illumination and enlightenment. Paul told the Philippians that God is the one who gives us the will or the desire and also the ability *to do of his good pleasure.*[12] Through the Holy Spirit, God makes it possible for us to understand, to know and to do what He wants us to do.

The psalmist prayed, *Thy hands have made me and fashioned me: give me understanding, that I may learn thy commandments.*[13] This is the work of the Holy Spirit. He is really the Teacher. Jesus told His disciples *The Holy Spirit, whom the Father will send in my name, he will teach you all things.*[14]

The Spirit's activity in teaching is twofold. First, He helps the learner to understand. Understand what? The facts of his Bible? No, for the facts of the Bible are there on the printed page for a person to study as he would any other book. The Holy Spirit's working is not a shortcut that eliminates work on the learner's part. But the Holy Spirit works in helping us to understand the *meanings* of the facts found in the Bible.

Second, the Holy Spirit helps the learner to take the facts that he now understands and apply them to his life. The Spirit makes the learner willing to take what is written, and with understanding apply it to his circumstances each day. To go back to Figure A, it is the Holy Spirit who, in the context of Christian learning, enables us to move from the simple handling of facts at the *familiarization* level to the application of their meaning at the *responsibility* level. This is His activity within the learner.

The working of God's Spirit is also evident in the dynamics of the class. Insights and learning do not come to the learner exclusively from the teacher. They can also come from other members of the group. A comment shared by one student can bring insights to others within the class. The teacher may also find that he is learning from the wisdom and experience of his students. It is the working of the Holy Spirit in the group as a whole that brings understanding. It is His activity that takes a new understanding and puts it into action.

The Holy Spirit is also at work in the life of the teacher as he prepares and presents the material. The Spirit gives understanding and illumination as the teacher studies the material. He gives inspiration concerning creative ways to present the lesson and to involve the students in the study. He gives a sensitivity to the needs of the students, enabling the teacher to structure the lesson to bring it on that collision course with students' needs. He motivates the teacher to be a learner himself, seeking new and better ways to communicate with his students. The Holy Spirit gives understanding of the different perspectives of the youth and adult cultures. He also gives the teacher fresh insights from the Word and ways to apply those insights to the needs and interests of the youth he is leading.

The work of the Holy Spirit is not limited to the student. The Holy Spirit gives the teacher the desire and the ability to lead today's youth in the process of change and learning. Youth are looking for involvement and for meaning in life. This means the teacher of youth must resist the temptation to limit his teaching to the lecture. He must lead youth to the level of exploration and responsibility where they can work with meanings and be involved in the life-changing process of learning.

CHAPTER FOUR

LEARNING WITH THE TEACHER

Someone once described the dedicated schoolteacher as a person who has no sense of humor and no outside interests. Many of us have had a teacher like that, and we can testify that anyone who fits this description is not one who is exciting and who inspires life-changing attitudes.

What *does* make a good teacher—specifically, a good Sunday school teacher? What qualities must a person have to lead students in the process of learning described in the previous chapter?

THE TEACHER'S CALL

How does one know that he is called to be a teacher of youth? Or called to any task in the church? Can one be sure of a calling? If a person could be sure that he was called, he might depend more on God's ability to equip him. Just what is a "call"? Does one hear a voice calling him as Samuel did? Or is it a more dramatic experience like Paul's on the Damascus road?

First, there are certain basic principles. One of these principles is that we are all called to be disciples of Jesus Christ, to be His followers. This is the meaning of discipleship—to follow Jesus as both Lord and Saviour. It includes the idea of discipline, of being obedient to His will. Everyone who names the name of Christ is called to this position. Obedience means the desire to know what God wants you to *do,* to know what area of ministry He wants you to be involved in. Obedience means that you start moving toward that area of ministry, open to any changes that He might want to make.

In your search, you'll finds lots of help! The visitation committee is certain that you are the one they need to help them in their work. The nursery department is convinced that theirs is the area that needs you most. The pastor says he sees in you the qualities needed for the work of a deacon. The youth minister feels confident that you could best be used in the area of teaching youth in the Sunday school. All these opportunities are available. Which one is God's choice for you?

Who is right? How can you decide? This certainly is not what is meant by a call! It is more like mass confusion. How can you move from your willingness to obey Christ to a sure knowledge of the area of ministry that God has for you?

Paul seems to have anticipated this problem as he describes the church as the Body of Christ. He speaks of this in several places (1 Corinthians 12; Ephesians 4; Romans 12:3-8). If you are to understand your area of ministry, you need to see the interrelationships within the body of Christ.

There is a variety of spiritual gifts, or functions, in the body of Christ. Just as there are two eyes, two ears, a nose, two feet, four fingers and a thumb on each hand in our physical body, with each working in a different way, so also in the body of Christ there is a variety of gifts or ministries.

In the three passages previously listed, you will find about eighteen gifts, depending on how you divide several of them. These are not talents, like playing the piano or singing, but are "ministries." Some of these are sign-gifts, such as the gift of tongues, of interpretation of tongues, miracles and healing. For our purposes here, we will limit our discussion to the other gifts, the gifts of service. These include pastors, evangelists, giving help, showing sympathy, administration and teaching.

Along with the principle of variety, there is also a universal distribution of these gifts in the body of Christ. Every Christian has been given a spiritual gift. If you have received Christ into your life as Lord and Saviour, then you have been given a spiritual gift of service! This gift of service is your *calling!*

But the question still remains—"How do I find my

calling?'' We have just changed the wording so that we now ask, "How do I find my spiritual gift?''

DISCOVERING YOUR SPIRITUAL GIFT

Let us first look at Romans 12:3-8. As Paul introduces the subject of spiritual gifts in this passage, he begins with the admonition to make a *sane estimate of your capabilities*.[1] You begin by looking carefully at yourself. Several options for service are open. You can serve on the visitation committee, work in the nursery, be a deacon, or teach youth in the Sunday school. Paul says that the first step is not to look at the options, but to look at yourself and your abilities. How has God put you together? What would you really enjoy doing? Be honest! Not "What *ought* I to do?'' but "What would I really *enjoy* doing?'' Your work in the body of Christ should be an offering of joy, an act of celebration, not some drudgery that pushes you to the edge of nervous collapse.

Note that nothing has been said about being qualified. That is not the question at this point. You begin by evaluating your feelings and abilities to find out where you would enjoy serving. Along with this step you find out what would be involved in each choice; in other words, you make an effort to be more familiar with all of the facts. If you feel drawn to working with youth, before you make that decision you should do some observing of the youth programs, talk with some other adults working with the youth department in the Sunday school, and find out from the youth minister what will be expected of the person taking this position. Perhaps even a trial run at helping another teacher might be arranged.

Along with investigating and observing, you make it a prayerful concern that God would guide you in your choice.

The second step in discovering your gift is in verse 6: *And since we have gifts that differ according to the grace given to us, let each exercise them accordingly.*[2] If in the process of evaluation, observation, investigation and prayer, you feel that you would enjoy teaching youth, then the next step is to start teaching. You tell the youth minister that you are available to begin. But just as in physical exercise, you do not go all-out the first time. You need training. So you study and start learning all you can about teaching youth. You have become *familiar* with the basic information. You have moved to stage II, the *feedback* level, by your response to offer your service. Then you start to *explore* by serving as a substitute, or assisting another teacher. Or you may learn by "in-service training" by taking a class of your own. With the help of the department leaders, you move through the exploration level to full *responsibility* as a teacher of youth. You are excercising your spiritual gift.

Unfortunately, the body of Christ too often looks rather flabby. We have failed to seek and discover our spiritual gifts and therefore we have failed to exercise them. As a result, what should be the muscle of the living church has turned to fat. We must discover and exercise our gifts. And just as we prayed in searching for our gift, we must pray in exercising our gift.

Once you have moved out in faith by exercising what you believe to be your gift, the third step is the *confirmation* of that gift by the results. These "results" are hard to define. It might be the response of the class to your teaching—the encouraging comments that you get from individuals in the class. It could be numerical growth. Or it may simply be the sense of satisfaction that comes after the class session—the satisfaction that it was a good session with lots of involvement by the students and good discussion that says you are "coming through."

What if there is no confirmation? What if you find total frustration? Make sure that your frustration does not come from a lack of training, or failure on the part of the departmental leaders to clearly define your task. But if everything has been right and you still do not find this confirming result, then move back to the first step and reevaluate. Stepping out in faith sometimes includes making mistakes. Do not hesitate to correct these mistakes and move on!

At long range, your spiritual gift will be confirmed when it accomplishes the purpose of spiritual gifts: *to equip*

God's people for work in his service, to the building up of the body of Christ.[3] The spiritual gifts are given to all of God's people in order that they be able to minister. Spiritual gifts are given to equip *youth* for their work in God's service, to the purpose of the building up of the body of Christ. This is why we teach youth. The purpose is cyclical. We teach youth so that they mature to the point of teaching others and finding their place of ministry in the body of Christ. We are trying to help each other attain *to the unity of the faith, and of the knowledge of the Son of God, to a mature man, to the measure of the stature which belongs to the fulness of Christ. As a result, we are no longer to be children, tossed here and there. . . .*[4] This is the goal of the learning process in Christian education.

What are the results in your own life as you find your spiritual gift of service? There is a sense of adequacy. You now understand how God can equip you for the job He has called you to do. It is a "spiritual" gift—the Holy Spirit is at work in and through you.

Sometimes we think that the Holy Spirit is looking for empty vessels. So we sit around trying to empty ourselves. We empty our heads waiting for the Holy Spirit to fill in the blanks. But the Holy Spirit is looking for *fit* vessels! As you discover and exercise your gift, you become fit to be used by the Spirit of God. You become fit by doing all you can in preparation, confident that the Spirit will saturate all your efforts with His power. This gives you confidence. And when you are confident that you are in the place God has for you, and that His Spirit is at work in you, you can be a "real" person, honestly growing and learning with your students.

This attitude of openness lets you abandon that "air of authority" that has so often surrounded teachers. The Scriptures are the ruling authority, and your responsibility is to direct students into the Word of God to find that true authority—not to be an "authority" yourself.

It is a glorious and awesome calling, to be a teacher. If God has appointed you to be a teacher of youth, then exercise that gift in the boldness of faith and in the confidence that God will equip you for the task.

THE TEACHER AS LEARNING LEADER

As you exercise your gift as teacher, what is to be your role—your method? Recognizing that you are part of the body of Christ, and that you serve as a teacher of youth for the purpose of the growth of that body, you see yourself functioning as a part of the great team effort. The members of the body are to function together for the common goal of growth. And your role as a teacher is to work toward that goal with the other members. You are not alone in this effort. In fact, others are helping you in your growth within the body. Perhaps a better title to describe the role of teacher is the term *learning leader.*

This term combines the idea of leading students with the idea that the leader, too, is learning. To be effective with a group of young people in a class situation, you must be involved along with them in the process of learning at the level of *responsibility.* The old axiom, "Teacher, Know Thyself" is changed to "Teacher, Teach Thyself!" Howard Hendricks, professor of Christian Education at Dallas Theological Seminary, often says that when he stops learning on his own, he will no longer function as a teacher. The learning leader is constantly open to new and fresh insights, open to the teaching of the Holy Spirit in his own life. Once he has the attitude that he has arrived, that the material is fixed in his mind and he has it all down pat, that is the point at which he ceases to be effective as a learning leader. The old idea of "teacher" still carries with it the concept of a "funnel-type" lecture, where the teacher is the source of all knowledge, and simply pours it through the funnel into the minds of the students. So we use the more descriptive term, "learning leader," for he leads himself and others in the exciting venture of learning.

The learning leader meets with his students so that they can move together in the joint venture of discovering what God has to say to them. The leader becomes a "player-coach," to use Trueblood's term.⁵ He is the coach, but he is also a player. As a player, he too is learning. As the coach, he knows the directions and the roads to use in order to arrive at the goal. He has the information, but he seeks to assist his students to find the answers on their own. He seeks to be an enabler. He tries to create a "discover-it-for-yourself" attitude in the minds of his students.

The role of the learning leader is to stimulate and motivate the student to move through the stages of learning on his own. A good coach pushes his players just enough to keep them motivated. If he pushes too hard, he discourages them. He makes suggestions. The pitching coach on a baseball team will demonstrate how the young pitcher can hold the ball better. The coach will suggest a change in the pitcher's windup that will improve his pitching. But the coach does not go in and pitch for him. This shows us that a good learning leader avoids telling the student what the student can learn for himself. He never does what the student should and could do in the learning process.

How does this work? Does it mean that we never arrive at conclusions or give any answers? Look at the pitching coach again. What does he do? He could have told the young player, "You've got it all wrong, kid. Do it this way." But the good coach would make suggestions in this way: "Why not try holding the ball like this?" He would demonstrate what he means and then let the player respond and explore the possibilities of that approach. The good coach is there to guide and to provide help when problems arise. The learning leader's role is similar. He suggests possible answers to questions, along with suggestions as to where the student might find more information. He might demonstrate how he deals with a certain problem in his own life, then suggest to the student ways to discover the application of these principles.

The learning leader stays with the student through the process, giving assistance and guidance when needed. He leads his students to conclusions and applications, but he does not spoil the joy of discovery by spelling out all the answers. The principles that the student discovers for himself will become a part of his experience more consistently than the answers given by an authority figure.

The learning leader's role is also to structure the time so that people can learn. He uses methods that will put some of the responsibility on the student. He makes sure that more than enough content is available to the learner.

But the learning leader can face the same frustration as the bewildered parent whose child has rejected him and everything he stands for. The parent provided a car, food, money and every *thing* necessary, but the child's response is still rejection. The missing ingredient is almost always personal involvement. As a learning leader you can provide content, motivation, good methods and environment and an exciting class session: but unless you are personally involved with your students, it will all fail.

Sometimes adult teachers of youth consider themselves responsible only for those 30 minutes on Sunday morning. They come to dispense pearls of wisdom to their students and wonder why their pearls are rejected. The reason: there is little or no personal involvement in the life of the students.

The true learning leader, the real player-coach, will get to know his students. He won't stop at knowing their names and where they go to school: he will get to know them as individuals by spending time with them. One man spends over twenty hours a week with the guys in his tenth grade class. He visits them at home, or sets up a time to meet with them and talk. He gets involved in their lives, sharing their problems, encouraging them and praying with them. He may not use all the best methods in the class, but he is a great learning leader, for he is leading those boys in learning how to follow Christ. One of his former students recently returned from four years in the Air Force. The young man told the teacher how the principles he had learned from their times together had given him stability in his faith so that he continued to grow as a Christian during his years in the service.

If meaningful learning is to occur in the class situation, the learning leader must invest more than 30 minutes a week in the lives of his students. He needs to get with them on retreats, show up at social functions, appear at school activities and spend time on a one-to-one basis with them. This personal involvement becomes the foundation for the group learning experience on Sunday mornings.

The role of the learning leader requires stimulating and coaching the students to learn on their own; setting the proper environment for learning to occur; and getting involved in the lives of the students.

YOU TEACH STUDENTS!

Obviously, in the type of teaching described here, the center of focus moves from the lesson to the learner. The learning leader is "learner-centered" in his approach. He does not teach the lesson, he teaches students. They work together in a learning experience. The teacher takes the curriculum materials, the teaching methods and the room environment, and seeks how best to use them to create a *learning* situation—not just a *teaching* situation. He has in mind the individual needs of his students as he prepares to create a situation in which the process of learning is free to proceed.

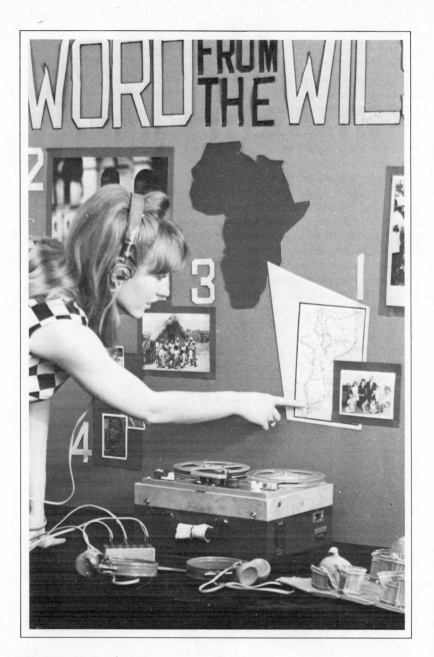

CHAPTER FIVE

ORGANIZING FOR LEARNING

WHAT ARE YOU TEACHING?

A lesson on a particular topic? Or students? There is a lot revealed in the way you answer that question. If you are merely teaching a lesson, then it does not matter if anyone shows up: you would get satisfaction from simply presenting the material. That statement is a little exaggerated, but it makes the point. You are either lesson centered or learner centered.

If you teach students, then everything becomes a tool helping you to create exciting and meaningful learning experiences for you and the students. You look at the curriculum material as a tool, seeking better ways to use it with your class. You choose methods carefully. You learn how to use audio and visual teaching aids to add variety and interest to your presentation.

Even the time becomes a tool. Many Sunday school workers cry that an hour is not enough—"What can you do with just an hour?" The creative learning leader asks instead, "What can we do to make sure that every minute of the hour is put to use in the learning experience?"

Some Sunday schools do not have an hour, while others may have 75 minutes. Some teachers may get only 10 to 20 minutes of class time, while others flounder around trying to fill in 60 minutes or more. The actual amount of time will vary from church to church. For our purposes here, we refer to the Sunday school hour as the total time available on a Sunday morning.

SCHEDULE

There are two basic approaches to the time schedule. One is the traditional plan with opening exercises held first, either for the whole Sunday school or for individual departments. This we will call *Plan A.* The other schedule uses large group meetings and small group meetings with a variety of possible arrangements. This we will call *Plan B.*

PLAN A

Traditionally, the youth department's Sunday school session has been made up of two parts: the worship assembly, either with everyone in the Sunday school or as a department, followed by the class session. And these two parts always seem to assume that order. Then there may be a concluding departmental meeting on special occasions.

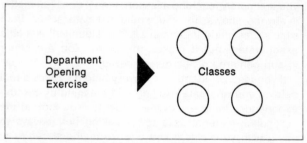

Department Opening Exercise → Classes

The departmental meeting was probably originated to include elements of worship. The program consisted of songs, announcements, an offering, and a devotional talk by the superintendent. On special occasions, there may be a guest speaker, and perhaps a birthday offering once a month.

This kind of program planning (Plan A) has its problems in relating to the Bible study material in the classes and little was done to tie the two parts of the program together until recent years.

During these opening exercises, the departmental leaders often have to urge the teachers to keep their kids in line. Discipline is a problem. And observation may reveal that very little worship is taking place. The song time is a great opportunity for teens to catch up on the latest news from a friend. And if the young people are careful, they can whisper the rest of the news during the offertory.

Observant departmental leaders often try to add variety to the opening exercise. They plan special programs that involve the youth in presentation and planning. They try to tie in the opening time with the class time as much as possible. There are a number of youth departments that have made this opening exercise a meaningful experience for their youth.

To do this, the superintendent becomes aware of the lesson material, knowing the lesson and unit aims and objectives. More time is spent in planning for speakers, films, and other methods of presentation. Coordination is achieved through planning with the teachers.

Plan A can be effective in the youth department of the Sunday school if the departmental workers are willing to make it work. But there are still serious limitations in this plan.

PLAN B

This recommended approach, called the "total hour" plan, involves the use of *large groups* and *small groups.* The large group is approximately the same as the departmental grouping, and the small group is the class situation under the leadership of the teacher. We change the names of the groups for several reasons, one of which is to disassociate this plan from former practices.

In this Plan B approach, the leaders of the assembly time and the class time are partners in planning for a total hour approach. Everything that happens in that hour relates to the aims and objectives of the lesson.

In planning together, the departmental leader and the teachers plan for the small groups.

The large group is used when the purpose involves communicating information quickly and efficiently through a speaker, a film, a multimedia presentation, dramatic or musical presentations, or group of speakers. The large group is also used to share insights gained in the small groups.

The small groups are used to provide maximum interaction among group members. Small groups provide an opportunity for the learning leader to guide the thinking and activity of the group and to evaluate responses.

The planning of the total hour for Sunday morning will usually include a variety of methods, some calling for large groups and others applying to small groups. Small group and large group sessions are grouped into various formats depending on the total hour lesson plan. Here are six possible arrangements:

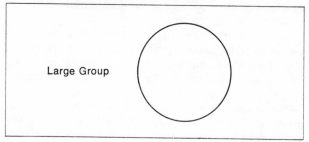

Large Group

The students stay in the large group for the entire hour. This would only happen on special occasions, such as a special film or speaker, or a dramatic or musical presentation.

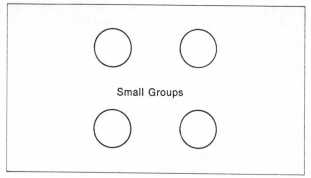

Small Groups

Here students remain in the small groups for the entire hour. Again, this would not be used very often, especially with younger youth. Careful planning, using several methods, would be required in order to use this format. This might be done with an inductive Bible study, research project, or a creative art project such as a collage or mural.

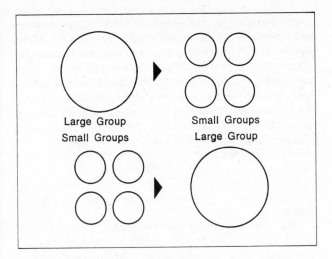

Large Group
Small Groups

Small Groups
Large Group

Here the large group session may either precede or follow the small group session. There are a number of possible uses of these arrangements.

Information could be presented in the large group. Then discussion would follow in the small groups, using a variety of methods. Or a Scripture passage could be discussed first in the small groups and then the large group could meet for roleplaying, a panel discussion or an interview.

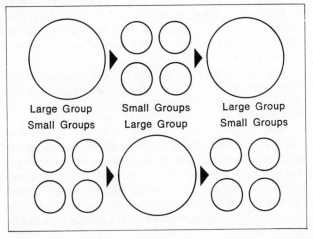

Large Group
Small Groups

Small Groups
Large Group

Large Group
Small Groups

These are other possible combinations of small and large groups. The time allotted to each segment can vary according to your purpose. In procedure number five, the first large group session might last only five minutes, giving the departmental learning leader time to present the problem to be studied in the small groups and the assignment for the final large group session.

Procedure six could be used when you want the small groups to meet first to prepare a special presentation for the large group. Following this presentation in the large group session, they would return to the small group to discuss or further study the material.

Within these six variations there are innumerable ways to use a variety of methods to involve your students in the learning process.

The choice of arrangement and the choice of methods is made by a team effort involving teachers and departmental leaders. This will require at the very minimum a monthly departmental planning meeting. You might call it the Sunday School Workers Conference, The Sunday School Council, or simply a Unit Planning meeting.

At this meeting, workers should come prepared to plan, not merely to find out what to do. They will come already familiar with the material and aims of the study unit. If they make adequate preparation, the planning for the unit can be accomplished in an hour or an hour and a half. If these meetings are held monthly, brief check-in meetings should be held each week after the Sunday school hour to make sure that everything is in order for the next week.

The best method of planning, however, is weekly planning sessions. This allows you to evaluate the previous week's learning experience and to plan the next session in light of this evaluation. If you cannot have the ideal weekly departmental planning session, then meet monthly with the weekly check-in. If you decide on unit planning, then your meetings would meet according to the length of the unit. It is not a good idea to meet less often than monthly. It is almost impossible to work as a team for the total hour on less than monthly planning meetings. The weekly check-in can be made immediately after the Sunday school hour, at postmidweek service coffee, or by phone. Its purpose is to confirm assignments and to consider any modifications in the original planning.

GROUPINGS

Most youth programs are considered successful on the basis of quantity of participants rather than on the quality of learning taking place. But if we measure success by the amount of positive change taking place within the group, rather than the size of the group, we raise a question about the "large" group. How large is the large group? Is its application limited to the large church?

For our discussion we define the large group as a range between 25 and 40. When the large group reaches a maximum of 35 or 40, you would divide the group and create two large groupings. These are attendance figures, not enrollment, and would of course refer to average attendance for several Sundays.

The 25-40 range is ideal. If you are working in a small church with a budding youth department, your large group might be as small as 10 to 12. It is considered a large group because it is made of two or more small groups.

Perhaps an illustration would clarify the distinctions. We define a small group as between 2 and 10, with 8 as the ideal. You are working in a new church and have 2 members in your senior high department. This is the beginning of the small group. Because of size, you are limited to procedure two—all small group. Because you are a dynamic and hard-working learning leader with the spiritual gift of teaching, there is a response. The class begins to grow. In two months, you are averaging between 8 and 10 each Sunday.

At this point, you look for another teacher, and divide your class into two small groups of 4 or 5. Now you have a large grouping—the two classes which make a department. And you have two small groups.

You continue to grow, dividing the small groups when they reach 8 or 10, until you have four small groups, and a large group attendance averaging between 35 and 40. Now it is time to divide the large group into two large groups of 18 to 20, keeping the small groups between 8 and 10 as a maximum.

This could continue as long as you continue to grow. The principles are keeping the large group between 35 and 40 as a maximum and the small group between 8 and 10 as a maximum.

Why? Because 8 to 10 are the maximum number of people for meaningful interaction between group members. If you try to use small group methods with more than ten people, it becomes easy for several members to sit on the fringe and not get involved in the process.

When the large group exceeds 35 or 40, it becomes difficult to administer. Individuals tend to get lost in the crowd. When the large group goes above this number, the number of teachers increases, complicating the team concept necessary for the total hour plan.

But what about the excitement created by a mass group of youth? Some large churches take great pride in their huge Sunday school classes. There is value in this size group that is related to peer feelings. But educationally, groups of mass proportions usually are ineffective. Perhaps the mass group concept can be promoted in some other phase of the youth program.

FORMING THE GROUPS

As your large groups increase in size and number, you face the problem of grouping the young people by grade and sex. There is no simple solution.

Based on the varied needs of youth, the basic division which should be made in every case is to separate the junior high from the senior high. Where this division is made would be dependent upon where the public schools in your area divide the junior and senior high levels.

Regarding the division of classes, the following guidelines are suggested: Seventh and eighth grades should be divided into small groups by sex. This is based on the different social needs and maturity levels of boys and girls at this age. If you let them sit as they want to at this age, you would almost always find the boys grouped together on one side, and the girls in another group.

Ninth graders still are not sufficiently comfortable with each other to say that you should always mix the sexes. The best advice is to continue to separate them by sex unless their maturity level indicates otherwise.

With tenth graders, the choice would be to mix them by sex unless their level of immaturity indicates otherwise.

There is seldom any reason to separate eleventh and twelfth graders by sex.

In the smaller churches, it would be better to mix seventh and eighth grade boys together rather than to create a seventh grade or eighth grade class mixed by sex.

	7th	8th	9th	10th	11th	12th
1.	___	___	___	___	___	___
2.	_____		_____		_____	
3.	_____		___	_____		___
4.	___	___	_____			
5.	_____		_____			
6.	_____			_____		

The chart shows possible grade divisions depending on the size of your group. If possible, the best arrangement is either separate departments for each grade, or departments for two grades together. According to the development of the adolescent, the ninth grader will be more compatible with the tenth grader than with the seventh grader. And the tenth grader is more like the ninth grader than like the twelfth grader.

The various groupings on the chart are placed in order of recommendation. According to your individual situation, try to achieve a grading program as high as possible on the chart.

PERSONNEL

Just as there is a pattern for dividing the group as it grows, there is also a pattern for adding workers in the growing department.

In the original small group, you have the teacher, the learning leader. When the group grows to 8 to 10, it is divided and another teacher is added. Two small groups make a large group or department, but there is no separate departmental leader or superintendent yet. One of the teachers takes this responsibility, working closely with the general superintendent.

When you have three or four small groups with teachers, you need a superintendent. His responsibility is to guide the department teachers in their role, to work with the general superintendent, to recruit the necessary teachers and to be involved in planning the total hour approach, sometimes helping with the large group assignment. It should be noted that the department superintendent is not solely responsible for the large group activity. Since this is a team effort, individual teachers might also take responsibility for the large group session.

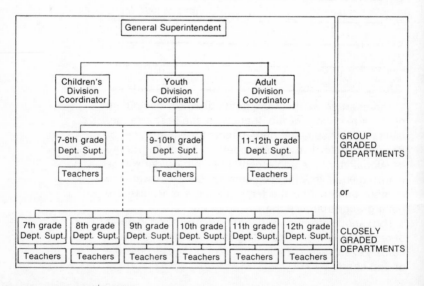

As you continue to grow, you will come to the point of dividing departments (large groups). With two departments, you have a "division." Just as two small groups make a department, two departments make a division. If there are four or more departments within a division, a divisional coordinator should be added. This is a position of overall administration in conjunction with the general superintendent.

For example, in the youth division, you might have a seventh and eighth grade department, a ninth grade department, a tenth and eleventh grade department, and a twelfth grade department. You need a divisional coordinator to work with your departmental superintendents, assisting them in their work and coordinating their work with the rest of the Sunday school.

Secretaries should be added when you have two or more small groups. As the department grows, you might also add an outreach leader, who will assist in contacting visitors and assigning them to particular classes. He would also work at contacting absentees, through the teachers. He could work creatively at planning various fellowship and outreach activities for the department. His knowledge of the department would make him an excellent substitute teacher when needed, or a new departmental leader when the department grows to the point of division.

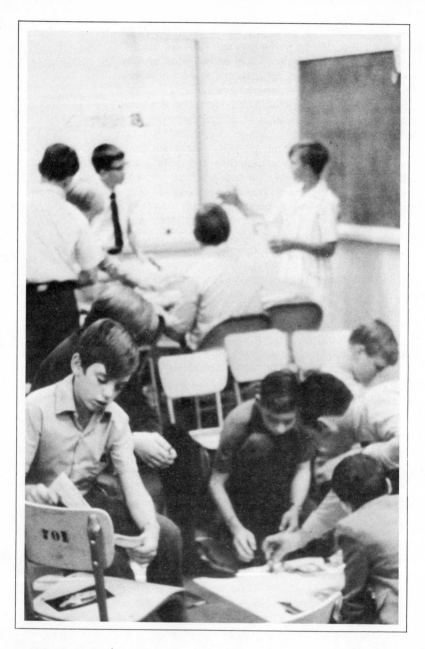

CHAPTER SIX

THE LEARNING ENVIRONMENT

The old saying that first impressions are lasting impressions is especially true when it comes to the youth department rooms. The physical appearance of your room conveys a wealth of information about the way you and your church feel toward youth.

Not only does the condition of the facilities say something about the owner, it also affects the quality of the learning experience. If the room is clean, bright and cheerful, both teacher and learner are stimulated to a more positive class session. This chapter will consider some of the attributes of a good learning environment. (For a more detailed study of both facilities and organization, see *Ways to Plan and Organize Your Sunday School* [*Youth*].)

ROOM ARRANGEMENT

First look at the room. Space requirements vary according to which expert you talk to. The range generally runs between 15 to 25 square feet per person. This means that the ideal room size for the ideal department would be about 1,000 square feet, or a room about 25 feet by 40 feet. This would provide adequate space for both large and small group activities.

The floor should be covered with an easy-care material which also absorbs sound. More and more churches find commercial grade carpeting provides the easiest and best floor covering to maintain. Walls should be clean and colorful. There should be adequate electrical outlets around the room to avoid the need for long extension cords.

Since the room will be used in a variety of ways, and probably for several different groups, stacking or folding chairs provide flexibility. If fold-up desk arms are available, they help provide a studious atmosphere, and are expecially helpful when methods such as inductive Bible study or creative writing are used. The ready availability of folding tables will assist in preparation for creative art projects, or other study activities.

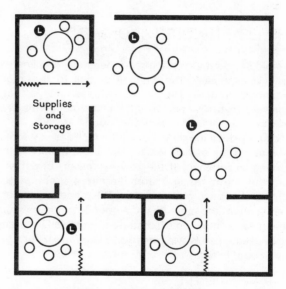

Open Room Arrangement

Keep in mind that the arrangement of the chairs is a part of the appearance of the room. Chairs carefully arranged in tight rows convey the idea of a rigid learning situation. If chairs are arranged in a semicircle, or in groups of four, a more relaxed atmosphere is created. Arrange the chairs differently every other week or so just to let everyone know that things are happening around the youth department. Care in planning the arrangement of chairs communicates a concern for the total learning experience that will not be overlooked.

A table by the door provides a place for the secretary to work, greeting and recording members and visitors as they come in. The offering plate or envelopes could be on this table, solving the question of when to take the offering. Since announcements no longer have a special spot on the program, you might consider printing up a "scoop sheet" with announcements. Make the sheet available at the table either before or after the Sunday school hour.

The piano should stay in the room even though it is not used every Sunday.

MATERIALS AND EQUIPMENT

The equipment necessary will vary according to methods used and the resources available to your Sunday school. Some equipment is basic. We have already mentioned folding or stacking chairs and tables. If you cannot add the folding arms to provide a writing surface, make lap boards available when needed.

Chalkboards are another basic equipment need. The most versatile type rests on a stand with rollers. With this, you can make any side of the room the front by moving the chalkboard into place. Or you can make a hanging chalkboard which uses hooks placed at intervals around the room.

Projection screens, too, should be movable. Or you can use blank wall space to project on, although the color of the wall might create a problem. Easels should be available for flipcharts or small chalkboards in the small group sessions.

A good guide to equipment is to keep everything *out* of the room that does not add to the study. Those things in the room should be portable, giving you a greater degree of flexibility in teaching and planning.

One semipermanent addition to the room is the resource center. This could be a shelf or table with resource books, including several Bible dictionaries, one-volume commentaries, Bible atlas, a number of modern translations of the Bible, and other resources needed for the study unit.

Storage area should be provided nearby for materials needed for creative art projects, group writing, spontaneous dramas, and for tables and extra chairs. This could also store extra chalk, chalkboards, easels and other equipment when not in use.

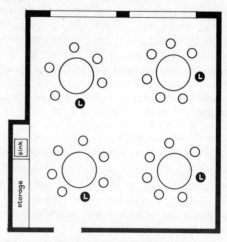

Assembly/Class Arrangement

What we have presented is the desired facility. You probably already have a building and room, and they may not sound at all like what we have described. Perhaps you have a fairly large room with a number of small classrooms attached. Then use the large room for large group activities and the small rooms for the classes. It might help create a team feeling if the doors were left open, or even removed. This would give better control in shifting from small to large group and back.

Perhaps all you have is a large room with no classroom space. This is not a problem, provided you have three or more small groups. You can put your small groups into the corners of the room, as shown here. Sound is no problem, for the buzz of three or more groups will not be distracting to the discussions.

Look at your facilities imaginatively, and seek to incorporate as much as possible into your present arrangement. If your facilities are totally inadequate, you might need to look around for other possibilities. Carefully consider all the possible solutions and then act on the best ones.

FOOTNOTES

CHAPTER 3

1 · Marshall McLuhan, *Understanding Media: The Extensions of Man* (New York: McGraw-Hill Book Co., 1964), pp. 23 ff.

2 · Martha M. Leypoldt, *40 Ways to Teach in Groups* (Valley Forge: Judson Press, 1967), p. 17.

3 · George B. Leonard, *Education and Ecstasy* (New York: Delacorte Press, 1968). The whole book is built on this theme and makes an interesting study.

4 · Leonard, *Education and Ecstasy,* p. 18.

5 · 2 Peter 3:18, *King James Version.*

6 · Carl R. Rogers, *Freedom to Learn* (Columbus: Charles E. Merrill Publishing Co., 1969). Chapter 14 deals extensively with this level of learning.

7 · Col. 3:16, *Revised Standard Version.*

8 · Roy B. Zuck, *The Holy Spirit in Your Teaching* (Wheaton: Scripture Press Publications, 1963), p. 9.

9 · Phil. 2:13, *The New Testament in Modern English,* copyright J. B. Phillips 1958.

10 · Ephesians 4:15, Phillips.

11 · Donald M. Joy, *Meaningful Learning in the Church* (Winona Lake: Light and Life Press, 1969), pp. 43 ff.

12 · Phil. 2:13, *KJV.*

13 · Psalm 119:73, *KJV.*

14 · John 14:26, *RSV.*

CHAPTER 4

1 · Romans 12:3-8, Phillips.

2 · Romans 12:6, *New American Standard Bible* (La Habra, Calif.: Foundation Press) © 1971 by the Lockman Foundation.

3 · Ephesians 4:12, from *The New English Bible.* © The Delegates of the Oxford University Press and the Syndics of the Cambridge University Press, 1961, 1970. Reprinted by permission.

4 · Ephesians 4:13,14, *New American Standard Bible.*

5 · Elton D. Trueblood, *Company of the Committed* (New York: Harper & Row Publishers, 1961).

PART III

YOUTH—THE METHODS WE USE FOR TEACHING

CHAPTER SEVEN

PUTTING AN HOUR TOGETHER

"WHERE DO I BEGIN?"

Did you read that with a feeling of anticipation? Are you anxious to put all of these ideas together into a lesson plan that will help you lead your students into an exciting learning experience? The purpose of this chapter is to help you get started and guide you toward that objective.

Since we have become "learner centered" rather than "teacher centered," the obvious starting point is with your students rather than with the lesson materials. This represents an *attitude* in your mind as you approach the materials, and it defines your perspective in terms of your students. What are their needs? What problems are pressing in on them? Where are they in their spiritual and developmental growth? How did they respond to the last class session? This kind of questioning helps to shape your attitude as you begin preparation for the coming class session.

The teacher's manual then becomes a *resource* in your preparation; your attention is still focused on the student and his needs. Unfortunately, some teachers have their eyes only on the teaching manual, and as a result are teacher centered. Instead of using the manual as a tool and a resource for creating an exciting atmosphere for learning, they handle the manual as if it were a script. It is *not* something to be read to the class, or to be covered down to the very last point in the class period. It has been designed to help you decide how you will lead your students in learning. When you are finally in the class with your students, the session depends on what you have in your heart and mind and how you intend to communicate it.

AIMS AND OBJECTIVES

When you pick up your teacher's manual, your first task should be to gain an overview of the quarter's material. In the introduction, there will usually be an explanation of what the course is all about. What is its purpose? Is it a topical study or a study of a Bible book? If it is a study of a Bible book, does it survey the whole book, give a chronological study of highlights, or look at topics within that particular book? Ask yourself some of these questions so that you can get the feel of the material and the general aims of the quarter's topic.

Once you have the overall picture, you will probably notice that the material is divided into "units." These units are usually arranged in blocks of three to five lessons each. You might consider the unit titles as the main points of the outline of the course. These units help you break up the quarter into workable sections. At the beginning of each unit, there is usually an introduction which presents the main purpose and aims of that unit.

With the unit structure, each unit has specific aims and objectives. The teacher is encouraged to plan each lesson as an important part of the overall unit aim. With a block of three to five lessons, the teacher is working with a manageable amount of material, and can look ahead and plan more than just Sunday-by-Sunday sessions. This adds continuity to the learning experience.

If we consider the unit title as the main point in an outline, then the individual lessons become subpoints in that outline. The lesson aims become supports for the overall objectives of the unit and of the quarter's material.

What really is a lesson aim? Is it any different from lesson objectives? No, not really, for they both refer to the desired results of spending time together in a learning situation. A more technical term would be to call them educational outcomes. They express the intent in the mind of the author of the material. They tell the main idea that was in his mind and what he hoped to accomplish in the learner through the material.

But since the curriculum materials are written for

thousands of teachers across the country and even in other parts of the world, it is difficult for the writers to meet the specific needs of *your* students. Sometimes several lesson aims are printed at the beginning of the lesson, giving you a choice of the most appropriate aim for your class. But even these may not be specific enough. So your next task, after thoroughly reading the materials and the Scripture passages, is to restate the unit aims and the lesson aims in terms of the students in *your* class. You might use a lesson planning sheet such as the one illustrated below.

LESSON PLANNING SHEET

Lesson # _____ Date _____

Unit Title _____

Unit Aim and Purpose _____

_____

_____

Lesson Passage _____

The central idea in this passage is _____

_____

_____

What would I like my student to KNOW, FEEL and DO as a result of this lesson?

KNOW _____

_____

FEEL _____

_____

DO

_____

MAKE YOUR AIMS SPECIFIC

You begin with the printed aims. Keeping in mind the purpose of the unit and the needs of your students, you adapt the lesson aims to fit your class. It may seem redundant to write out the aim of the unit each week.

But it serves as an important reminder of where you are heading. This part of the planning sheet is designed to help you arrive at specific lesson aims:

Let's take an example from what might be a course on John for junior highs. The unit title is "A New Thing." So we write this title after "Unit Title":

Unit Title: _A New Thing_

The next step is to fill in the aim of this unit, which we find stated in the introduction to the unit of study.

Unit Aim: _To identify the events John uses to show that Jesus introduced a new way of living with God._

These unit aims form your guideposts as you approach the individual lesson on John 2. After reading through the passage of Scripture and the material in the teacher's manual, you try to narrow it all down to one central idea.

To be able to do this, you must understand the central truth in the biblical passage to be studied. This means that you will study carefully both the passage of Scripture and the resources available (teacher's manual and other resources at your disposal). Read over the passage several times, rethinking in your own words the main idea in the passage. What is the overall emphasis in these verses? Compare your thinking with the lesson material. Look at the main idea of the key verse. Do these agree with your impressions?

It is important to have the main idea in your mind, but even more so to put it on paper. Your statement should be written carefully and clearly, for it provides the basis for building your lesson plan. In John 2, the central idea seems to be the authority of Jesus. He possessed authority over nature, turning the water into wine. He exercised authority over men as he instructed the servants to serve the wine and as he ordered the money changers out of the Temple. After a careful study of John 2 and the teacher's manual, you might write in your lesson planning sheet the central idea this way:

Lesson Passage _John 2_

The main idea in this lesson is _that Jesus had great authority which was obvious to those He met._

When you have written down this central idea, you have a general direction in which to move. It also helps solve the problem raised by this teacher. . . .

How do you select the important items from the excess of material in your teacher's manual? A good manual will present far more material than you can possibly use in one lesson. This is done purposely to give the teacher as much background and as many resources as possible to build a lesson that is tailor-made for *his* students.

In the passage we are looking at in John 2, the teacher has two different events in the life of Jesus which make the same point—He possessed great authority and men saw this authority. The teacher can choose which event to study. He does not have to spend time on both, or he can quickly look at one event and then look in depth at the other part of the passage.

The teacher is able to make this choice because he has found the central idea and stated it. But is this fair to the passage or to the lesson material? A better question would be "Is this fair to the student?" And the obvious answer is yes, since we are leading students in a learning experience, not teaching lessons.

Now you are ready to move on in your effort to make your aims specific. Martha Leypoldt has pointed out that the changes taking place in a learning situation fall into three catagories: knowing, feeling, and doing.[1] Changes take place in our knowledge about a subject, in our attitudes and feelings toward it and in what we do as a result. It is much easier to make specific lesson aims for the areas of knowing and doing than for feeling. These are called *affective* aims and deal more with the internal responses of the student than with his overt behavior. Since they are related to attitudes and feelings, it is difficult to state exactly what results are desired and to know whether the goals have been achieved.

A large area of Christian education works in the area of feelings and attitudes. We can depend on the working of the Holy Spirit to accomplish within the learner these feeling and attitude goals and objectives. But since changes in feelings and attitudes are usually based on changes in knowledge and understanding, and lead to changes in what we do and how we behave, it is a good practice to fill in objectives for all three areas: knowing, feeling and doing.

In your lesson on John 2, you might fill in the three areas like this:

What would I like my students to KNOW, FEEL, or DO as a result of this lesson?

> KNOW? *That Jesus had such great authority that people obeyed Him, even if they didn't know Him.*

> FEEL? *A sense of awe and wonder at His tremendous authority.*

> DO? *Identify areas of their lives not under the control or authority of Jesus Christ.*

These are your desires for the class session. They form your specific aims and objectives, the desired results of spending time together in a learning experience.

There is no advantage in keeping your lesson aims a secret from your students. However, it is advisable to exercise care in how you share lesson aims related to feelings and attitudes. You don't want a student to fake the desired response in order to please you.

Since we are working with student-centered learning experiences, it is helpful not only to share your desired objectives with the members of the class, but also to work together in setting some of the aims and objectives which you hope to reach together. Let's take an example of sharing your aim. In our lesson on John 2, you could share the "doing" aim. As you approach the end of the session, you might simply say, "One of the things I would like you to *do* as a result of our study today is to take a moment and consider some of the areas of your life which are not under the authority of Jesus Christ." After students have thought for a minute, you might ask them to help you set a goal: ask what you and they can do together to help each other turn over these areas to the control and authority of Jesus Christ. They might suggest taking time right then to have conversational prayer for each other. Or they might propose a time of silent prayer of dedication, with time at the beginning of the next class session to report to the others how God has worked during the week.

This teamwork in setting goals is also very helpful when planning the unit study, since it gives you insight into the students' needs and interests, and insures that you will be leading in the right direction. Class discussion of goals during the presentation of the overview of the material is one way to involve the young people. Or you may set up a planning session with several of the key members of your class and discuss possible goals and objectives for the unit.

We have spent some time discussing lesson aims and objectives. Their importance cannot be overstressed. The practice of writing your own lesson aims to fit the needs of *your* students is like working over a road map to choose the best route to reach your destination. Good, clear aims also help you in your next task, which is to figure out *how* to get to your objective. What methods do you choose?

CHOOSING METHODS

Your destination has been picked—you have your aims and objectives in front of you. Now comes the choice of routes—which road to take? Which method to use? Sara Little points out that we need to exercise great care in choosing our methods. She makes it clear that "method in itself communicates content."[2] This is another way to say that the *way* you present the material can drown out the content that you are trying to communicate. On the other hand, it can add support to what you are saying. If you only lecture, every Sunday, directly from the teacher's manual and with a detached attitude, you are communicating to your students by the misuse of the lecture method. Your detached lecture says you do not really care if anyone hears: at least you get to talk. You need to be careful to use methods in a way that will assist you in reaching your objectives.

Real effectiveness in teaching methods results only when a teacher comes to class with a full heart. Methods are not a cure for poor or inadequate preparation. They are the result of spending time throughout the week becoming familiar with the Scripture and resource materials. They arise out of a deep concern to guide your students into the heart of the material, to experience changes as a result of an encounter with the one who is the life-changer—Jesus Christ.

The careful choice and use of methods can also create and stimulate interest on the part of your students. The right methods can get your students involved, taking them from the role of listener to one of actively digging into the Scriptures. They can create the desire to explore and study intensely in order to consider all of the possible options.

Perhaps in preparing a class session, you feel that most of your students will have their minds made up on the issue before the class even begins. Perhaps the lesson on John 2 will have a problem getting started because of the rejection of authority by many youth today. So you choose to face the problem by starting the class session with a debate, presenting the pros and cons of doing away with all authority figures. Several students are asked to prepare their side of the issue before the class session. And sure enough, your students come with their minds made up, and after the "pro" side of the argument is presented, everyone cheers in agreement with the idea of doing away with authority figures.

The student assigned to present the "con" side of the issue struggles to get started, and finally presents his side, raising a number of important questions that the others had not considered. Perhaps some get angry, but several get agitated enough to start digging for some answers, especially in light of the authority of Jesus Christ in their lives.

The wise learning leader will not solve the issue on the spot, but will direct the students to resources where they can discover for themselves the possible answers. Perhaps they will arrive at the same answer they started with, but they will be learning. They will *change* from having an "opinion" to being able to support a position. This search can take the form of a "research and report," which would be used to stimulate the learner to further study and also provide further involvement of the class when the report is made.

Methods can also stimulate the learner to make practical applications of the material being studied. Sunday school teachers have had a tendency to depend solely on the Holy Spirit to make the applications from the lesson passage. The teacher's task has been to "present the truth" and leave the rest to the Holy Spirit.

It *is* the task of the Holy Spirit to apply the truth of Scripture; but why not enjoy the thrill of being a partner with Him by using methods to help apply the truth of the Scripture.

When John studies prayer in his seventh grade class, the Holy Spirit can work within his life and apply some of the principles discussed during the class session. But the learning leader can assist by making a project assignment at the end of the session. He could ask John and the others to make a list of specific prayer requests and to apply several of the principles they have studied when praying for these requests during the week. The opportunity to report the results at the beginning of the next class session can reinforce the application of these principles in the future. Application results from the careful selection of a teaching method.

As in the case of John, the learner reaches the desired objectives because he gets *involved* in the learning process. Some methods lead to greater involvement than others. This is graphically portrayed in the "cone of experience" developed by Edgar Dale,[3] which we have adapted in Figure B.

VERBAL AND VISUAL SYMBOLS

Student learns in the "abstract." Visual symbols include chalk-board, diagrams, maps, charts, etc. Verbal symbols include the most abstract of all learning experiences—reading a book or listening to a lecture.

AUDIO/VISUAL PRESENTATIONS

Student learns by seeing or listening, but not both. For example, he listens to a record or radio program or a tape. Or he may look at a silent film, a slide presentation, filmstrip, or a series of still photographs.

AUDIO-VISUAL COMBINATIONS

Student learns through combination of audio and visual elements as in television, motion picture, filmstrips with sound recording or slides with sound. Student may become deeply involved but is still experiencing indirect learning because he is watching representations of real life.

DEMONSTRATIONS, FIELD TRIPS, EXHIBITS

Student learns mainly by observation as he watches someone show him "how to do it" or as he visits a place or tours a point of interest, etc. He has a "direct experience" but is more the observer than the participator.

CONTRIVED OR DRAMATIZED EXPERIENCES

Student gets directly involved through situations devised to get him to participate by talking, moving about, writing, drawing, etc. Some ways to give these "made up experiences" include: discussion of a case study, question and answer session following a lecture, buzz group discussions and reports, panel discussion, brainstorming, role play, dramatic skit, operating a model or mock up, going through a simulation (dry run of the "real thing").

DIRECT PARTICIPATION

Student learns by doing. Has "real life experiences" with responsibility for outcome. Actually builds, makes, teaches, produces, manages, etc.

INDIRECT EXPERIENCES

DIRECT EXPERIENCES

ABSTRACT

CONCRETE

THE "CONE OF EXPERIENCE"

According to Dale, the lower on the cone you go, the more direct is the involvement of the learner in the process of learning. And the more direct his involvement, the more concrete and obvious the effects will be in his attitudes and actions.

At the top of the cone are verbal and visual symbols, and the methods associated with them. These promote learning in the category of unreal and indirect experiences. A large portion of teaching, both in public schools and Sunday schools, is done in this indirect area. The best learning takes place at the bottom of the cone, through direct experiences where the learner actually tries something on his own. The more involved your students get in the class session, the more the learning experience will be real to them.

Dale also says that as we move lower on the cone, many of the higher factors on the cone are still involved. Almost any method on the cone presupposes the use of verbal symbols.

Keep a copy of the cone of experience on your desk as you prepare your session and as you choose methods. Try to use as much as possible those methods that fit into the lower end of the cone.

BUT HOW DO I CHOOSE?

You now have several aids on your side as you begin to choose which methods to use. The central idea of the lesson is your guide, and the lesson aims are essential helps in choosing methods. The cone of experience is a valuable resource to refer to when making choices. And your understanding of the methods described in the next chapters completes the picture.

The next part of the lesson planning sheet is designed to help you arrive at a choice of methods.

Begin by listing all the possible methods that might be appropriate to this lesson and its aims. List them according to methods for large groups and methods for small groups. (The distinction between these will be found in chapters 8 and 9.)

You choose your methods by answering the question, "What Bible learning activities and methods could be used to help my students reach the goal listed under know? Under *feel?* Under *do?"* As you consider each of the aims, you choose methods that will possibly assist you in teaching. For example, you see that under *feel,* you have written something like, "to feel a sense of awe and wonder at the tremendous authority possessed by Jesus." What method could you use to help your students *feel* this? It might be a roleplay of the situation, or a creative writing assignment in which the student describes how he would have felt if he were one of the characters.

Do this also with your aims written after *know* and *do.* When you are finished, this section might look something like this:

What Bible learning methods and activities could be used to best help my student reach these goals?
In *Large* Groups?   In *Small* Groups?
roleplay   *creative writing*
debate   *buzz groups*
dramatic reading   *inductive study*

At this point you will have too many methods. This is good. It gives a choice as you create your lesson plan with a step-by-step procedure of learning activities.

KNOWING	FEELING	DOING
Book Report	Brainstorming	Demonstration
Film	Buzz Group	Field Trip
Interview	Case Study	Project
Lecture	Circle Response	Work Group
Panel	Couple Buzzer	
Question and	Creative Art	
Answer	Creative Writing	
Research and	Debate	
Report	Drama	
Symposium	Discussion	
	Listening Team	
	Inductive	
	Bible Study	
	Role Play	

On page 88 you will find a list of methods adapted from Martha Leypoldt's book. [1] The list shows which methods are most effective for the three categories of learning. This list is only suggestive. Many of the methods listed under "Feeling" also assist in the development of knowledge, as do those listed under "Doing." The process of learning is ultimately concerned with producing change in actions, in behavior. Those methods listed under "Knowing" provide the basic information needed, but are less likely to produce changes in behavior than the methods listed under "Feeling" and "Doing."

The categorization of methods can also be tied into the four stages in the process of learning. Those methods listed under "Knowing" would probably fit best in the *Familiarization* stage of learning, where we seek to communicate the basic information. Lecture is one method used at this level, along with panel discussions, book reports, or research and report assignments.

The *Feedback* and *Exploration* stages of learning would include methods listed under the "Feeling" category. *Feedback* would use such methods as buzz groups, film talk-back, circle response, listening teams, and brainstorming. *Exploration* would use methods such as inductive Bible study, roleplay, debate and symposiums. *Responsible* learning would use methods such as action projects to be handled outside of the class session, preparation of class presentations, or student teaching assignments.

Once you have selected possible methods, there are several other factors which must be considered.

THE SIZE OF THE GROUP WILL BE
A FACTOR IN YOUR CHOICE

Six to eight is the ideal size of the small group, thirty to forty the size of the large group. Some methods work best in the small groups, others work best in large groups, and some methods will work in any size group.

If your youth department is small, with only a total of five or six present on your best Sunday, most of these methods can still be used in your learning session. A symposium might be hard to achieve, and a panel would be a problem if there were more people on the panel than in the department. But just about every one of these methods can be used and adapted for the small department. On the other hand, if your youth department is large, you will find it necessary to create the small groups to use many of these methods.

A study of the relationships between people in a group shows that meaningful participation on the part of the individual is best in the small group of three or four. The larger the group, the more the possibility of individuals being left out of the learning process. This is why it is recommended that you set a maximum size on your classes and on your department.

The **size of the room** is another factor, as is the **time** available for the learning experience. Some methods require more space, such as roleplaying, group drawing, and work projects. Other methods require more time. Couple buzzers take just a few minutes, whereas group writing, debates and field trips require a substantial block of time.

Resources are another factor. If you want to use a film, do you have a projector available? If you are going to do group writing, will tables be available in the classroom? If you are to lecture, will there be an overhead projector, chalkboard, or flipchart for you to use? If a research and report assignment is to be given, are there books available for the young people to use in their research?

The **ability** of your students is another important factor. Some of these methods require a certain level of maturity on the part of students. It would be quite difficult for a seventh grader to present one side of a debate. Most seventh graders have difficulty thinking in terms of concepts and opinions; they are more comfortable with facts. Debates work best with older youth. Using puppets or models might have a greater appeal to the seventh grader than to the high school senior. These limitations will be considered when we look more closely at the different methods in the next chapters.

THE LESSON PLAN

You have your goals and objectives defined in terms of the central idea in the passage. You also have a list of possible methods to use to reach these goals, and you are aware of the factors involved in using the different methods. Now you are ready to put it all together into a lesson plan.

MY LESSON PLAN

How will I get their attention? _____
_____
_____
_____

How will I lead them into the Bible Study? ___
_____
_____
_____

How will I guide them into making personal application? _____
_____
_____

Note that your lesson plan is not simply an outline of ideas, but is a progression of learning activities. You begin with getting the attention and interest of the learner. Let's say you are still working with the lesson on John 2. How do you get the attention of your students? What method could you use to get them into the atmosphere of learning? You look at the list of methods you have already listed, and you make a choice and write it out, something like this:

How will I get their attention? *With a debate, resolved: Do away with all authority figures. What about the abuse of authority? Won't some authority arise to fill the void? —Look at some current issues involving authority?*

You choose to use the debate, and you have listed the question to be discussed and some suggestions of how to introduce the debate. You might also pencil in names of possible debaters.

Do the same with the next two questions:

How will I lead them into the Bible study? _In a buzz group—"Why did the servants and money changers obey Jesus? How is Jesus' authority different from anyone else's? Is it? How do you know?_

Take the time to evaluate your plans. Anticipate problems. What if there is no response in the buzz groups? How will you reword the assignment to get them started? What alternative plan could you have ready in case they cannot see the authority of Jesus expressed in these passages? Perhaps you could do a dramatic reading, and at the point where Jesus gives the servants the order to serve the wine, you could have one of the servants tell Jesus _No!_ Then send them back to the buzz groups to find out why the servant did not really say _No!_

Asking yourseif these kinds of questions during your preparation will help you lead the learning experience. It is much easier to anticipate different responses than to panic in the face of an unexpected response. Evaluate your plans for the conclusion of the lesson as well.

How will I guide them into making personal applications? _Ask them to prayerfully consider their own lives and list on a sheet of paper areas not under the authority of Jesus. Perhaps share an area and then pray for each other._

Again, evaluate your plans and anticipate any problems. What if no one is willing to share with the group an area of his life not under the control of Christ? What other approach might be used?

If you are working with other teachers in a department, this lesson plan will form the basis for your weekly or monthly planning session. If each teacher prepared these ideas, there would be a wealth of possibilities for an exciting learning session. If you are the only worker in the department, you will be on your own; what you have written on the lesson planning sheet becomes the skeleton of your final plan.

The notes you actually take with you to the class session will be written on another sheet of paper. They will be built around the three questions of the "lesson plan" section of the planning sheet. You will need to add how you will move from the attention activity to the Bible study activity and finally to the application stage. You will want to include ways to introduce the different methods, questions to be used and any illustrations you want to remember.

There is one more section on the lesson planning sheet. This includes the six diagrams of the possible total hour arrangements. Filling this in will help you visualize how the different parts of the hour will fit together. In our lesson on John 2, the pattern would be number 4—Large Group/Small Group:

Time Schedule:

Activity	**Activity**
#1	#2
Small Group _____	Large Group _____
#3	#4
Small Group _____	Large Group _____
Large Group _____	Small Group _____
#5	#6
Small Group _____	Large Group _____
Large Group _____	Small Group _____
Small Group _____	Large Group _____

There are probably as many suggestions for lesson plans as there are books on the subject. The best plan to take into the class session is the one that gives you confidence, helps you to be an exciting learning leader, and helps you to be open to the responses of the students. Whatever plan you use, it should include a way to begin the lesson, methods for moving through the various activities of the learning session, and a way to conclude the session and reach your desired aims and objectives.

Once you have finished the session, be sure to evaluate what happened. Spend some time reflecting on the responses of the learners to the different methods used. Did the methods create the interest you thought they would? Did the students respond? Did they get involved as you planned and hoped they would? Were you underprepared for any particular method? Take the time to reflect on the session, making notes about the methods that will help you use them better in the future.

If you are really bridging that culture canyon, your ears will be open to the comments of the students and their reactions to the different methods used. Be open to their reactions, carefully weighing them in light of your purposes and aims with the group. This evaluation should be done as soon as possible after the class session, and forms the beginning of your preparation for the next session.

The well-prepared teacher is one who has evaluated past sessions, studied and prepared throughout the week rather than in a jam at the last minute, and carefully thought through his plans to lead the learners to the desired objective. This kind of preparation gives him the confidence to begin the session, the resources to be able to change his plans in the middle of the session if necessary, and the spiritual sensitivity to know when and how to conclude the learning session!

It is an awesome task to lead today's youth in learning experiences but God has promised to abundantly bless the faithful servant, the growing learning leader!

LESSON PLANNING SHEET

Lesson # _____

Date _____

Unit Title _____

Unit Aim and Purpose _____

_____

Lesson Passage _____

The central idea in this passage is _____

_____

_____

What would I like my student to KNOW, FEEL and DO as a
    result of this lesson?

   KNOW _____

   _____

   FEEL _____

   _____

   DO _____

   _____

What Bible learning methods and activities could be used to
    best help my student reach these goals?

   In *Large* Groups?   In *Small* Groups?

_____

_____

_____

_____

MY LESSON PLAN

How will I get their attention? _____

_____

_____

_____

How will I lead them into the Bible Study?

_____

_____

_____

_____

How will I guide them into making personal application?

_____

_____

_____

_____

Time Schedule:

Activity   **Activity**

#1   #2
Small Group _____   Large Group _____

#3   #4
Small Group _____   Large Group _____
Large Group _____   Small Group _____

#5   #6
Small Group _____   Large Group _____
Large Group _____   Small Group _____
Small Group _____   Large Group _____

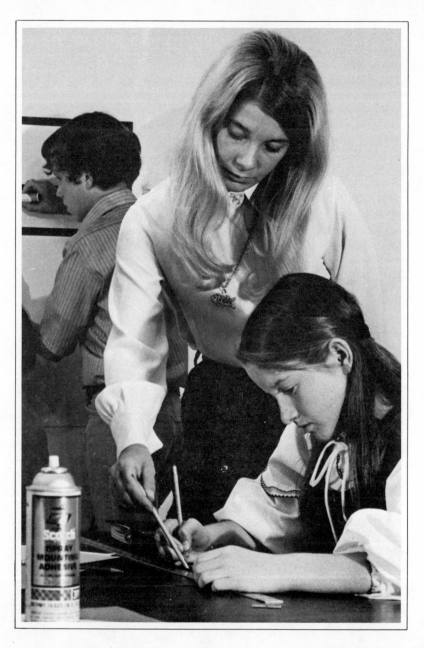

METHODS FOR SMALL GROUPS

The creative learning leader does not have to be skilled in all the arts of group dynamics in order to use methods successfully. If you are willing to take the necessary time for planning and evaluating, and are willing to experiment with new ideas and combinations of methods, you will discover that the time spent will be extremely rewarding. You will also find an atmosphere of openness, excitement and learning in your group.

Sometimes a teacher chooses methods because he mistakenly believes it will take less preparation time than putting together a lecture. But if you want to be a confident learning leader, you will find that most of these methods will take more preparation time, especially if you are going to be prepared for the unexpected. To lead an exciting learning experience takes time. It takes preparation time, it takes time in the class, and it takes time during the week getting involved with your students. But teaching is not just the act of a moment, when you walk into a classroom. It is the outpouring of your life![1] Take the time to understand the methods you choose and to prepare to use them effectively.

The methods described in this chapter are suggested for use in the small group. This was described in chapter 5 as the grouping led by the teacher, or the class session. It is to be distinguished from the large group, or departmental session led by the department director. Many of these methods require the large group session, either for preparing the learner for the small group experience, or to provide opportunity for the learner to report the results of his exploration.

With each method, you will find a cartoon describing how it works. Study these carefully, since they not only tell you the suggested seating arrangements, but also show the type of communication involved. If only the leader speaks, you will find a one-way arrow like this:

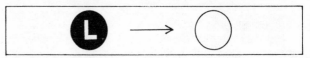

In some methods, communication will flow both ways between the teacher and group members, but not between group members themselves. This two-way communication will have a two-way arrow:

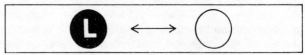

If the members of the group are encouraged to work together and discuss with each other as well as with the teacher, this multidirectional communication will have many two-way arrows:

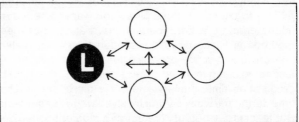

Sometimes it will be easy to recognize the leader in the diagram. At other times, you will not be able to tell the leaders from the learners. That is the way it should be, for the leader is a *learning* leader. But to help you recognize the leader's role, we will put an "L" on the leader like an ear, making him look like this:

Notice that we put the "L" where the ear should be. This is because the learning leader needs to be especially sensitive, hearing the responses of the learners as he carefully leads the learning experience.

BRAINSTORMING

The leader presents a problem or a question to the group. This method is especially helpful when the responses of the group seem to be caught in a rut.

As the problem is presented, the members of the group are to respond quickly with any answer or solution that comes to mind. It does not matter how appropriate the response may be. The object is to say what comes to mind and have someone write it down on the chalkboard, newsprint, or overhead projector.

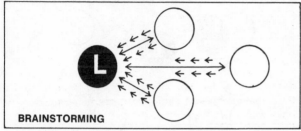

BRAINSTORMING

No evaluation is made of any response at this time, even though the response may seem far off base. One absurd remark might trigger an idea from someone else which may turn out to be the best response.

The leader should set a time limit for brainstorming, such as three minutes or five minutes. When the time limit is up, or when the responses slow down, the brainstorming stops and the evaluating begins.

If you have been brainstorming a problem or doing some planning, you might have to eliminate the least valuable answers or ideas. Then evaluate the remaining suggestions in order of importance, or arrange them in categories. After they are arranged, the group might consider how to put into effect the ideas suggested or apply the solutions offered.

Brainstorming can be used for problem solving, defining terms, planning events or lesson and unit aims, and reviewing previous material. In each case, the purpose is to come up with as many ideas as possible from the group members.

BUZZ GROUPS

This is one of the best ways to get the members of your class involved and become part of the learning process. The group is divided into small groups of from three to six persons each. A time limit is given, usually five or six minutes. (These groups were originally called Phillips 66, because Dr. Phillips of Michigan State started the practice of dividing an audience into groups of six for six minutes.[2])

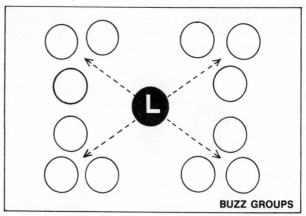

BUZZ GROUPS

The learning leader clearly defines the task to be accomplished in the buzz groups, making certain that the group members understand what is expected of them.

Give the group enough time, but do not let it drag out. Junior highs will have a hard time staying on the subject, especially if given too much time. Even senior highs should have no more than six to eight minutes, unless the problem is involved and requires more time.

The learning leader should suggest a method for choosing the buzz group leader and recorder. Some simple technique such as the one whose birthday is closest, or the one whose middle name starts with a letter closest to the first letter in the alphabet.

One of the problems with this method is the physical arrangement of the room. Chair shifting takes time. Careful arranging of the chairs before class will help. You might arrange the chairs in groups of five or six.

These groups can then form a circle to create the buzz groups. Or you can simply have every other row turn to the row behind them. Closeness of the groups to each other is not a problem, because everyone is tallking at once anyway and each group will be concentrating on its own conversation.

The learning leader circulates freely among the groups, offering suggestions and help when needed. He should be sensitive to the timing, calling the group back together early if the "buzzing" slows down, or giving more time when necessary. He should give a two-minute warning before calling "time," so each group can arrive at conclusions. After the groups regather into the large group, the learning leader will ask the leaders of each group to report to the others the results of their discussion.

Buzz groups provide an opportunity for everyone to be involved in the learning process. Valuable insights and information are provided, and in turn often provoke a lively discussion in the large group.

CASE STUDY

A case study is a true or a hypothetical situation that duplicates thinking or events common to the learner's experience. Members of the youth culture are concerned about the problems others face, and eagerly get involved in analyzing and solving the problem presented in the study.

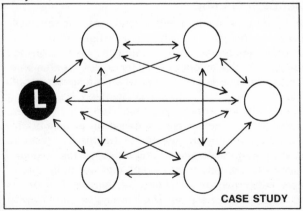

CASE STUDY

Case studies are often provided in curriculum material for youth, helping the learning leader guide the students in application of biblical principles to life situations.

The learning leader presents the case study, giving the necessary background information along with the various factors involved. Interesting ways to present the case study include using a tape-recorded presentation of the situation.

The learner listens carefully to the case study, attempting to see clearly the problem and possible reasons why it exists. Members of the group then suggest possible solutions to the problem, carefully evaluating each suggestion and its possible outcome. They should have good reasons for choosing the best solution to the problem.

The learning leader will guide the students by challenging their solutions and pointing out the strengths and weaknesses of their arguments. He will help them reach some conclusions. The purpose of the case study method is not only to analyze the problem, but to apply to the solution the biblical principles being discussed.

Case studies can be found in many sources other than the teacher's manual. Magazine articles and newspaper advice columns provide possibilities. If the case study is taken from a leader's personal experiences, great care must be taken not to break a confidence, even if the names are changed or disguised.

CIRCLE RESPONSE

This is a simple method with several uses. It is especially valuable when the subject is somewhat controversial, or when someone has dominated the discussion and you want to give an opportunity for others to participate. Circle response is also useful when a discussion gets rather hot and the learning leader feels he is losing control. The leader proposes a question to the members of the group. Each person is called on to give his response in turn (around the circle). No one can respond to any person's statement until his turn comes again.

This can be used to have each member of the group state either his understanding of the question or his response to the question. The learning leader may also call for a vote as to which side of the issue the person identifies with. The statements should not be addressed to any particular person, but might be imagined as being tossed into a "ballot box" in the center of the circle.

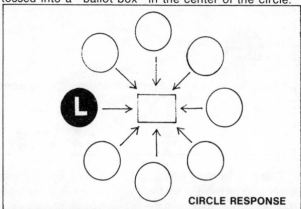

CIRCLE RESPONSE

This method is valuable in providing an opportunity for each member to participate by contributing his opinion. It also gives an opportunity for each member to consider the opinions of the others since he cannot respond until his turn comes again, or the discussion is reopened. It is a method that the learning leader should have close at hand to use when needed. It can also be used to open up discussion on a question.

COUPLE BUZZERS

This is similar to Buzz groups in purpose and method, but is limited to two people in a group.

It is used when there is not enough time for buzz groups, or when the leader wants to get the learners involved in the problem quickly. It provides an opportunity for each member of the group to be faced with the issue and to respond. It also helps get the individual members involved in the process of the learning experience.

The learning leader does not move among the groups, but is available for clarifying the problem if necessary. He defines the time limit, which can be anywhere from one to ten minutes. He gives a short warning before calling the couples back together to discuss their ideas.

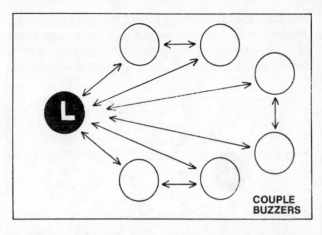

COUPLE
BUZZERS

This can be done with a small group of four or more. It can also be used in the large group, where the speaker requests the members of the group to pair off to discuss a question, and then have several relate their discussion before continuing the lecture. Since people merely turn to the person next to them, there is seldom the need to move chairs.

DISCUSSION

There is probably no more potentially valuable method of teaching than discussion. A discussion that is carefully planned and skillfully directed can change an ordinary class session into an exciting and lively learning experience.

Sometimes a teacher will try a discussion and fail, vowing never to use that method again. Or the teacher may be fearful of the questions that might be raised and therefore never even make the effort to try. Unfortunately, the students of such teachers miss the opportunity to internalize facts, ideas, and concepts and to wrestle with their meanings.

A discussion has been defined as "a cooperative search for truth as the group seeks solutions to a problem or question." There is interaction between teacher and students and between student and student. The learning leader is there to be a resource and a guide to keep things going.

The best physical arrangement for discussion is a circle, which allows members of the group to see each other. The beginning of the discussion may sound more like a question-answer session, with the teacher addressing questions to the group, and answers given back to the teacher. But if the questions are phrased in a way that defines the issue involved, the group will start reacting and the discussion will start rolling. There must be an issue involved. It just does not work to try and start a discussion on a point or issue where everyone is in agreement.

Even if you have an issue, sometimes youth may be in a mood that stifles good discussion, and you never get past the question-answer phase. Be patient and go on with the session as planned, and if you keep an atmosphere of openness and acceptance, your students will eventually open up. Avoid putting them down by criticizing their lack of response.

The learning leader should carefully plan the discussion questions so answers will have to be more than yes or no. Have another question ready in case students do not understand the first question. Or be prepared to reword it. This is not the time to lecture, so keep questions and comments short and to the issue.

Sometimes your discussion will be more exciting if you make advance assignments. For example, in a discussion on the inspiration of the Scriptures, part of the class might be asked to read some material based on your church's position. Others might be asked to read some material on opposing positions, while others are given the task of finding out what the Scripture itself says about inspiration. With this kind of research done before class, you can be sure of a lively discussion.

Some may object that it is too risky to let youth be exposed to the various other positions. But isn't it better to have them exposed in the context of the class session rather than later in some college classroom? If we are working with the truth, we have nothing to fear. Because we are handling God's Word, we come back to the biblical principles involved. The Bible, not the classroom teacher, is our authority, and we can trust the Holy Spirit to guide us in our study.

Another way to stimulate discussion is to show a picture and have the young people tell a story about what is happening in the picture. Several may suggest different ideas, or they may agree on one. This can lead into discussion of feelings, situations, biblical principles or other matters.

Once the discussion begins, the learning leader keeps the discussion on the track. Occasionally, you may find it necessary to tactfully ask a "happy wanderer" how his comments apply to the topic. Be careful not to appear shocked when he has an answer for you. If the majority of the group indicate their desire to take a tangent and discuss it, the learning leader should be open to this possibility.

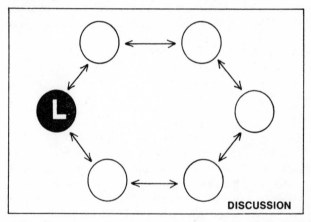

DISCUSSION

The learning leader should be sensitive to those not participating. In striving for balanced involvement, he might seek to draw the quiet members into the discussion unless it would embarrass them.

At times, the learning leader might quickly summarize the discussion to that point, or ask one of the members of the group to give a summary. At the end of the discussion, a summary should be stated, along with possible conclusions. If no agreement was reached, then a restatement of the issue and various possible conclusions might be given as a summary of the session.

Discussion will usually follow one of the other methods, such as buzz groups, case studies, open-end stories, roleplaying, or a short lecture. The main objective of a discussion is to encourage the group members to express their opinions. These opinions are open to change as other opinions are expressed and the discussion continues. Students need the assurance that they can express what they feel without getting blasted out of their chair by the learning leader. Leaders are to encourage expression as the beginning of learning, and then trust the Holy Spirit to do the changing and remodeling when necessary.

INDUCTIVE BIBLE STUDY

Through inductive Bible study the learner discovers the meaning of a passage of the Bible by seeking the answers to the questions, "What does the passage say?" "What did the author mean by this?" "Why did the author say it?" "What does it mean to me?" A good way to rephrase this last question is to have the learner ask, "So what?" and then look for the answer.

An inductive Bible study avoids using commentaries, but will refer to Bible dictionaries, Bible atlases, and concordances, and various modern translations. The primary resource material is the Bible itself. The objective of the study is to find out what the passage says and then to determine its application to life.

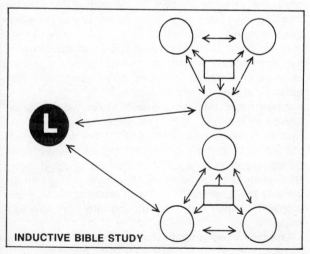

INDUCTIVE BIBLE STUDY

An effort is made to confront the plain sense of the passage without reading into it our preconceived ideas. In an inductive study, we try to draw out of the passage its apparent meaning and then to confront our own ideas with the meaning of the passage.

The learning leader will provide the necessary resources mentioned above. It is best to have tables for the members of the group, allowing room to spread out the various translations and resources. Groups of two or three work best during the study session, reconvening for discussion of their discoveries.

Some prepared questions might be available to help direct the group research. These can be the questions referred to in the first paragraph, but made specific by referring to verses or statements. For instance, in an inductive study of John 3:1-15, one of the study questions might be, "How might Nicodemus, a Pharisee, understand Jesus' use of the word *water* in verse 5?" You would need to have a Bible dictionary available to help answer this question. Or another question might be, "What was Jesus referring to in verses 14 and 15, and why did He use this illustration with Nicodemus?" These questions are designed to guide the learner's inquiry into the passage without giving answers.

Another method of digging for the meaning is to paraphrase a verse or section. Students put the passage into their own words, trying not to use any of the words already found in the text.

During the study and research time, the learning leader should be available to give guidance concerning choices of resource materials or to assist in finding cross-references in the Scripture.

When using this method with junior highs, careful choice of questions and of the Bible passage is important. Senior highs are better able to work with the ideas behind facts. But if you are working with junior highs, by all means seek to use this method of self-directed Bible study. If you have problems with the younger youth, simplify the passages and the questions, so they can discover on their own the meaning of a Scripture passage.

The time needed for this method will vary according

to the difficulty of the passage. In a simple study made for younger teens, 10 to 20 minutes will be enough time. For a more difficult assignment with older youth, and especially with seniors in high school, you could plan a study that would take 30 to 45 minutes or more. You should leave time enough at the end for the subgroups or research teams to present the results of their study to the rest of the group. Summarize and apply what has been discovered.

The hidden value of this method is that an exciting learning experience through inductive Bible study will motivate individuals to further study of the Bible on their own. Here is an excellent example of the method itself bringing about change in the life of the learner. Perhaps the revelation that he is able to discover meanings by studying the Bible inductively on his own will be a greater learning experience than the actual content of what he has studied.[5]

PROJECTS AND WORK GROUPS

Projects and work groups are distinguished from the other methods in that they go beyond the class time into the student's own time. In a project, the learner is working on the *exploration* or *responsibility* level of learning.

The learning leader provides leadership in determining the problem or issue to be studied. He will also give direction in the choice of resource materials and suggestions for the form of the completed project. As the group is divided into working subgroups, the learning leader will help each work group decide what part of the finished project they will prepare.

A group of junior high students were studying the Lord's Supper and baptism, the two sacraments or ordinances of the Protestant church. The class was divided into three work groups to prepare a presentation for a youth night at church. One work group decided to compare the two Protestant sacraments with the seven sacraments of the Roman Catholic church. Another work group took the assignment of explaining the meaning of baptism and the Lord's Supper. The third work group decided that they wanted to prepare a slide presentation of the symbols used to represent the sacraments and to tape the results of the other groups for a sound track to go with their slides.

Each group worked alone for awhile. Then they had a session together to share what they had prepared so far, and to make suggestions to each other about the finished project. The finished product was of real interest and help to the rest of the church and was a valuable learning experience for the junior highs preparing the program.

A group of older teens took a mission trip to work at an orphanage in Mexico. One of the fellows was interested in making a film about the trip, so a work group was formed to plan and create the film. They started filming in the parking lot as the group left the church. All weekend the camera cranked the film through, capturing various aspects of the weekend's work and of the cultural setting. The real work started after the trip was over and the developed film was returned. Hours were spent editing and cutting the film to present the desired message. The results were presented in a report session at a Sunday evening service, and the whole church was confronted by the weekend and its purpose.

A work group might be assigned the task of watching the TV program guide for material related to the study unit. If they find something of interest, a class social might be structured around the viewing session, with discussion following the program.

If you have students with special interests, such as photography or art, you can give special assignments to create murals, relief maps, and photographic exhibitions related to the topic of study.

Another project can be related to service or outreach. In seeking to apply the principles of a certain passage or unit being studied, a service project might provide opportunity for a real learning experience. Different work groups might plan the details of a day spent at the beach with an inner-city church youth group, or a service project at a mission church.

The opportunities are unlimited. More and more, we need to break out of those 60-minute sessions on Sunday morning and carry the learning experience into the life of the student during the week. Projects and work groups provide the teaching method to carry through this objective. Sometimes the Sunday school learning leader feels this type of activity should be delegated to the youth minister or to some other part of the youth program. This is unfortunate, for these are learning experiences which we should be actively leading. Of course, coordination with the rest of the youth program is necessary, but should not be an excuse for avoiding this type of involvement.

The project should not be considered finished until its results are evaluated by everyone involved.

TIME LINE

Learners work together to organize information that is related to a time element—the growth of the early church, the life of Christ, the history of the English Bible. They research the facts, then transfer them to a chart representing the progression of time. This is usually done with a long sheet of paper marked off by years, with the events marked at the appropriate points in time. However, other possibilities include a "clothes-line" sort of arrangement with colored paper clipped or taped to the line to represent years and events.

The time line may be developed in the small group, then displayed and explained in the large group.

QUESTION AND ANSWER

This method is probably the one most used in the learning experience—in fact, often neither the learner nor the learning leader is aware that a method of teaching is being used. It is one of the easiest methods you can use, but for it to be a vital part of the learning process, it must be used wisely.

In the diagram, you will note that the questions and answers are between teacher and student, not between students. It is important that when you ask a question, you try to choose a student who will not feel pressured or "picked on."

There is less involvement with this method, although the other students are involved to the degree that they are interested in how their peer handles the question. Keep in mind that question and answer is not a discussion, as some might believe. Leading a question and answer session is easier than trying to get a group of junior high or senior high youth into a discussion, though sometimes the question and answer time will lead into a discussion.

The secret to success with this method is in *writing* good questions. Some are to be avoided, such as leading questions like "Of course you all agree, don't you?" Little is gained in asking this type of question.

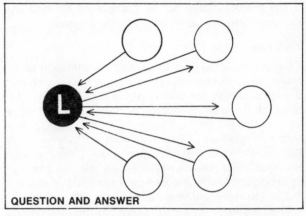

QUESTION AND ANSWER

There are two major kinds of good questions that a teacher can ask during an interesting question and answer session: factual and thought questions. The factual type of question will ask for definitions to words, such as *justification*. Or it might ask for a location or a name. Factual questions are usually the who, what, when and where type of question.

Thought questions are the best kind to use for they are designed to help the learner use the facts to draw conclusions, gain insights and understandings, and make applications. In this type of question you are looking for the why behind the facts. As a rule, these thought questions are harder to put into words, but are worth the time necessary to prepare them.

Before writing your questions, it is important that you know the material you intend to cover. This is so basic it almost sounds superfluous, but many a teacher will try to use questions to bluff his way through a class session. You cannot ask good questions unless you know the material.

Word your questions carefully and write them down on your lesson plan. Then evaluate each question by asking: Is it clear? Is it brief? Is it factual or thought provoking? Can it be answered with a simple yes or no? (If so, write an immediate "why" after the question.) Sometimes a good discussion can be started by asking, "Why do you say yes (or no)?"

Take your time when asking the questions. Give the learner time to think. This is not an inquisition or the witness stand, but a learning experience. If the student waits too long to respond, reword the question and ask someone else, taking the pressure off the first person asked. When seeking to draw the shy learner into the learning experience, ask opinion questions or use some of the easier, more obvious questions.

Work on getting the students to ask you questions. The action in this method goes both ways. Encourage questions by giving the class opportunity to ask them. Treat their questions with respect, seeking to answer directly, or promise an answer the next time if you are unable to answer.

Not every question can be prepared in advance. The questions that launch the session can be prepared in detail during your lesson preparation. But the guiding questions that "spin off" other questions depend on what is happening in the group at the time they are asked. These cannot be prepared in advance, but come from the general preparation of the learning leader. The discipline of writing out good questions in preparation will help you form good questions on the spot.

An alternate suggestion by Martha Leypolt[6] involves the learning leader preparing a mimeographed list of questions on the topic. These are given to the learners after an explanation of the procedure. The individual members of the class then ask the learning leader some of the questions from the sheet. The learning leader responds, and can in turn ask questions of the group members. This helps the shy member get involved and also guides the learning experience into areas of interest to the learner.

CREATIVE ARTS

Not everyone is an artist, obviously, but youth enjoy working with their hands in various art projects. There are several art forms which can be used with youth which get them involved on a feeling level in the learning process.

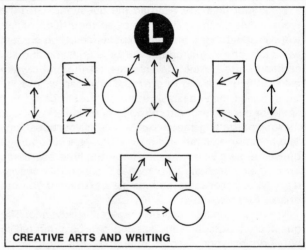

CREATIVE ARTS AND WRITING

The group is divided into small groups of three to five. You will need space along with tables, or large bare floor space. The objective in each case is to encourage your students to express their ideas in some art form.

BANNERS AND POSTERS

Felt banners and posters are popular art forms with youth. These take more time than is usually available on a Sunday morning, so would probably be more of a project or work group. The results are both decorative and instructive. The project can be assigned and discussed in a small group on Sunday morning and then carried out during the week at home or at the church.

The learning leader should provide suggestions as to

the general theme or topic. He can provide the necessary materials along with instructions concerning what is expected in the finished product.

Different colored felt should be available for the banners. Poster board, poster paint or felt tip pens provide the drawing materials for the posters. The finished products become related teaching tools in the unit study.

MONTAGES

These are fun to make and are often very revealing about the needs and interests of the youth. Group members can work individually or in small groups. Be sure you have enough room for them to spread out their clippings.

You will need to provide a large piece of butcher paper for each montage. Assign members of the group the task of bringing stacks of old magazines, preferably the picture type. You will need a pair of scissors for each person, and some paste.

Your students should skim through the magazines looking for pictures and captions which express their feelings about an assigned subject. A group of junior highs were asked to create a montage that expressed their answer to the question, "Who am I?" The results were in some cases superficial, but in others, showed a depth of expression.

This can also be a project done at home and then brought to class. Part of the learning experience comes as each student is given opportunity to explain the meaning of his montage to the others in the group.

DRAWINGS AND DOODLES

Drawings can be done in small groups with an appointed artist in each group. He can listen to the ideas of the different group members and then try to create a drawing that suggests their combined ideas. He would then explain the drawing to the other groups.

Doodles can be a fun way of expressing feelings.[3] Artistic talent is not required, only the willingness to move a pencil with feeling. Each group member is asked to try to enter into the feeling of the narrative in Scripture. Perhaps to try to feel like Mary and Martha as Jesus comes four days too late to heal Lazarus. How did they feel when they saw Jesus coming? Then how did they feel after Jesus brought Lazarus back from the dead? Try to doodle one or two drawings that express these feelings. The real value of doodles comes in explaining them to the rest of the group, describing how they express the feelings in the passage of Scripture.

MOBILES

A hanging mobile can be created to express the theme of the quarter with each piece of the mobile expressing the topic of one of the study sessions. This can be done at the beginning of the quarter, giving an overview of what is to come. Each group can create different parts of the mobile, which is left on display during the quarter as a teaching aid.

CREATIVE WRITING

You will be amazed at what your students can create in writing. Even though they will protest that they are not writers, if given the inspiration and opportunity they will produce some interesting results. (Students can write individually or in groups.)

OPEN-END STORIES

These are similar to case studies, except the situation is printed on a sheet of paper with space left for the student to finish the story. The learning leader may present the case with the background material and different factors involved. Then the story is given to the student. He reads the story, which just happens to break off at the crucial point. The learner's task is to finish the story, working out the situation.

When finished, the learner shares his "ending" with the class and also responds to the contributions of the other group members. The value of this experience is increased if the learning leader will briefly summarize the various solutions presented and ask for some possible applications of the principles discussed.

WRITING ROLEPLAYS AND SQUIRMY SITUATIONS

Roleplaying will be described in the next chapter under large group activities. The point here is to suggest that you have your students write out the roleplay situations and then either act them out themselves, or have another group act them out.

One group of junior highs, when asked to write a modern-day version of the Ananias and Sapphira event, came up with some interesting ideas. One class suggested a group of fellows working to raise money to send other kids to camp. The group raised $30 and gave it to one of their members to turn in to the youth director. But he only turned in $20. What happens when the others find out?

Or you might have them write some squirmy situations that confront the group with the point of the passage being studied. The lesson might be about Peter's vision of the sheet filled with different animals being let down from heaven with the command to *"Arise, Peter, kill and eat!"*[1] Peter finally gets the message that he is not to limit salvation to the Jews, for God is no respecter of persons. The writing assignment would be to write a situation that shows how we might be respecters of people who are different from us.

Again, the value comes in either reading or acting out what has been written along with discussion of the meanings involved.

IMAGINARY INTERVIEW

Imaginary interviews are simple to do. The students read the Bible passage assigned to them and then think of how an interviewer might approach the persons included in the incident and what questions he would ask. (Most students have seen television interviews, so they will be familiar with this approach.)

The students then determine the answers the interviewed person might give. In some cases they will find a direct basis for both question and answer in the text. In other cases, they may have to apply their own judgment and imagination to the text to determine answers. There is no right or wrong here, so no student needs to feel threatened about this type of work.

IMAGINARY DIARY

The young person reads the assigned passage, then

tries to put himself in the place of the suggested character. He uses his imagination to write a page that the person might have written in his diary that day. The biblical text provides the basic information, and the student uses his own judgment to fill in details of inner thoughts, feelings, reactions and conclusions.

The imaginary diary need not be long, but it should lead the student to deeper thought. There are no ready-made, right-or-wrong answers, so he must actually think.

Allow students to read their work to the class before the end of the session. Then collect the papers and read them during the week. Make encouraging comments on the papers and return them next time.

WRITE A NEWSPAPER ARTICLE OR STORY

In this method, the student writes a newspaper article based on the assigned text. He should write his article as it might have appeared in a newspaper the day after the event. It might be written from a neutral, objective point of view as a straight news item, or it might be written as an editorial or personal statement by someone who had met Jesus Christ and believed in Him.

The article won't need to be long, but it should include as many facts—the who, what, where, when, why and how—as possible. The sentences should be short and concise, the headline chosen appropriately. In some cases the biblical text will provide the material needed, while in other cases the student will need to use his imagination to fill in details around the information given.

Or the student may write a story based on the information in the assigned passage. He can use his imagination to fill in details of what led up to the biblical event or what followed. Since there is no right or wrong concerning these matters not recorded in the Bible, the student can feel free to suggest any reasonable "plot." This method will help the student get involved in the biblical narrative and understand the people as real human beings like himself.

One student, studying the story of Simon the Pharisee, Luke 7:36-50, chose to write why Simon invited Jesus to his house and what he did in the days and weeks following the incident. The student indicated whether he thought Simon eventually came to believe in Jesus or turned away and became one of those who sought Jesus' death.

GRAFFITI

A phrase such as "Happiness Is . . ." or "Thanks, Lord . . ." is written at the top of chalkboard or a large sheet of shelf paper. As students arrive, they are given chalk, pencils or felt tip pens and encouraged to write whatever they feel is appropriate to the theme suggested by the heading.

SONGS AND POETRY

Some members of your group may have poetic talent and can create some beautiful lyrics to sing or read. Encourage them to share their creations with the group. Provide opportunity and materials for this kind of writing as well. Other variations include writing stories, creeds, newspaper articles or prayers. Perhaps some will only write a sentence or two, but at least they are trying and thinking. Be sure to provide an opportunity for sharing and evaluation. The various contributions might also be arranged into a worship service or a youth night program for the church congregation.

These are methods designed for small groups. They have been selected because they are the easiest to use in the Sunday morning class situation. Once the learning leader is able to use these methods comfortably, other methods are available to him. Many of these are found and explained in some of the books noted in the Bibliography.

CHAPTER NINE

METHODS FOR LARGE GROUPS

The methods described in this chapter are designated for large groups—the department time. These methods are usually led by the departmental leader or someone chosen either by him or by the teachers at the planning meeting.

It should be noted that the distinction "large" is not primarily referring to numbers. If you are working in a small church, you would use these methods in what has been traditionally called the "departmental session" of the youth department. You will find they are easily adaptable to any size group.

DEBATE

This method is designed to present opposing views of a controversial issue. It is not recommended for youth under senior high age, although an informal approach which seeks to list the pros and cons of an argument might be used with younger youth. Those assigned to present the different positions on the argument must be able to handle logical reasoning, which is beyond the ability of most younger teens.

Not every topic of study will lead into debate. In order to use this method, there must be a clear issue with two different sides. For example, it would be difficult to have a debate during a study of Old Testament personalities. But a good debate could be developed in a study on morality. Or you could introduce a unit of study on witnessing by having a debate on the issue: "Resolved, that Christians should witness only by their lives." You would then choose one or two willing debaters for each side of the argument and they would research their position prior to the debate.

The departmental learning leader's task involves defining the issue for the group members and especially for the debaters. He can suggest possible resource materials, especially to the debaters who might be taking the side they do not really believe to be true. In advance of the debate, make sure the room is arranged properly, with a podium for each debater or team of debaters.

The general pattern to follow during the debate is to have the affirmative side of the question begin with a stated time limit. This is the "pro" argument. When time is up, equal time is given for the negative, or "con" position to present their proofs. Usually 5 to 10 minutes will be enough time for each side to present their positions. Then a brief period of time, about two minutes, is given for the "pro" team to give rebuttal, with an equal amount of time given to the opposing team for rebuttal.

Following the debate the departmental leader will either open the topic for discussion by the whole group, or will summarize the two positions presented and break the large group into small learning groups led by the individual teachers.

During the debate, the large group might be asked to write down the main points made by each debater. These notations would help form the basis for a good class discussion following the debate.

Some of your senior high young people may be on the debate team at school and will relish an opportunity to debate an issue of their faith. Others in your department might enjoy this method if given the opportunity. An excellent reference book for help in leading a debate is McBurney and Mills' *Argumentation and Debate,* listed in the Bibliography of this book.

Some guidance might be needed, especially if your debaters have little or no debating experience. You should check with them before the large group meets to make sure they have made adequate preparation. They should be able to clearly present their positions, defining terms and supporting their viewpoints. In rebuttal, they should challenge the arguments of the opposing side, defending and summarizing their own position.

This method is especially valuable as a learning experience for the debaters, and also provides a launching pad for some good discussion. It can also be varied by being less structured. You could divide the group into two teams and then list the supports for each side of the argument on a chalkboard. Or you can choose two debaters on the spot to present the sides of an issue to the rest of the group.

DEMONSTRATIONS

This is simply what it says: a demonstration of how to do something or how to apply a principle to one's daily conduct. One or more group members may present the demonstration.

For example, in a unit on sharing your faith in Christ with your friends, a demonstration team might show the large group how to create an opportunity in a conversation to share their faith in Christ. Or if the unit of study is on conversational prayer, a team might demonstrate how to pray conversationally.

The departmental learning leader introduces the demonstration with an explanation of its purpose and describes the steps to be shown in the demonstration.

Following the demonstration, the learning leader will again describe the steps involved and suggest ways to use what has been demonstrated. He might then divide the large group into small groups to carry out what has been demonstrated.

If the witnessing situation was demonstrated, the group would be divided into subgroups of two. Each subgroup would then carry out a similar witnessing situation, practicing on each other what has been demonstrated to the group. After the practice time, the group could be reconvened, or sent into their class groupings for further discussion of any questions or problems encountered during the subgroup experience.

The use of demonstration and practice gives the learner confidence in doing what is expected in the unit study. It also helps clarify any misunderstandings or problems which might develop if the learner were expected to implement the application on his own.

DRAMA

With drama, the material comes to life for the students. It can be either a well-planned production of a written play, or a spontaneous production created almost on the spot. One form of spontaneous drama is roleplaying, which we will look at separately.

There are a number of good plays available for youth to plan and present. Some require only two people, while others require crowds of youth to participate. The presentation would be considered a project: it would require careful planning with enough time for preparation in order to make the presentation at the right point in the unit study.

Good advance planning on the part of the departmental staff will include a polished performance of a play as a part of the learning experience. Usually, complete instructions for a planned production are included in the scripts.

PLAY READING

Not every play must be a production. Sometimes parts of plays can be used simply by having members of the group read the parts for the large group audience. The departmental learning leader could introduce the part of the play being presented, giving background material for the scene to be read.

This type of presentation does not require rehearsals, although a once-through reading before the meeting is suggested. Staging, costumes and lighting are unnecessary. And acting skill is not required of the readers.

Scenes can be lifted out of secular plays to illustrate a point in the learning experience of the group. Several resources for church plays are listed in the Bibliography.

Similar to play reading is *conversational Scripture.* This is used with narrative passages of Scripture, especially in the Gospels, or in the Old Testament narratives. Different parts of the narrative are assigned to readers. The passage is then read as though it were a play. This is done by leaving out the "and he said, . . ." from the conversation. This helps to bring the passage to life as it makes the interaction between characters clear.

SPONTANEOUS DRAMA

Following study of a story or narrative in Scripture, spontaneous drama makes the account come alive. Plans can be made in small study or buzz groups; then the dramas are presented to the large group. The entire process is informal, with no written record or script.

One group of junior highs were studying the book of Acts. When they came to the account of Saul's conversion, they decided to review the references to Saul earlier in the study as well as in this lesson, and then to act out the events in his life leading up to his conversion and his encounter with Ananias. They decided on three scenes: one when Stephen was stoned, another on the road to Damascus, and the third in the room with Ananias. After twenty minutes of discussing plans in the small groups, they met together again to present the three scenes.

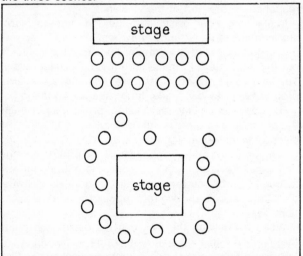

The whole process, from planning to presentation, becomes a part of the learning experience. A debriefing of the actors following the presentation would include a chance for them to share their feelings as they took the part in the play.

Another approach to spontaneous drama involves

enacting specific events in Scripture. A project work group could research the different aspects of such events as the Passover celebration, or the Festival of Booths referred to in the Gospels. Or they might research the various steps involved in the Old Testament sacrificial offerings, and then reenact these events before the large group. When these projects are approached with reverence, they become not only learning experiences, but worship experiences as well.

FILM TALK-BACK

There is an increasing number of short discussion films available at moderate rental price (or on a free loan basis from public libraries) which would provide excellent discussion starters for youth. Many filmstrips are designed for the same purpose, or for presenting information about a particular subject. The distinctive feature of the film talk-back is that it always provides for a response on the part of the viewers.

In planning a film or filmstrip, the departmental learning leader should arrange the room so that everyone has a good view of the screen. He should also check out the equipment to make sure it is in working order. The time spent making sure that everything is prepared properly will pay dividends during the presentation.

Before using any film or filmstrip, preview it carefully. If more than one person will be involved in leading the discussion, have everyone preview the film. This will also assist you in introducing the film to the group. Nothing dampens the learning experience more than for the leader to introduce the film with, "I don't know what the film is about, but we're supposed to look at it, so here goes."

When previewing the film, use the discussion guide that comes with it to help you frame some questions to pose to the group to consider while viewing the film. (If no guide is available, construct questions on your own.) Following the actual showing of the film these questions will provide the basis for buzz groups or discussion. If the meaning of the film or filmstrip is not clear to the group, you might consider showing it again.

Some films or filmstrips are designed to be stopped

at a certain point for discussion, and then started again at that point. When this is suggested, it is a good idea to follow this format for involvement. (It's also wise for the projectionist to practice this procedure in advance.) Other films will be shown straight through but the leader should have some plan for reaction by the group members.

INTERVIEW

Through an interview, someone who has a particular contribution to make can share his knowledge with the large group. Usually this is a person who has "expert" knowledge about the topic. The interview usually leads into a discussion among the group members, either in buzz groups or in class groupings.

The departmental learning leader usually contacts the person to be interviewed. He briefs the guest on the subject the group has been studying and the information he wants to cover with the guest. In some cases the leader will give the guest, in advance, a copy of the questions he plans to ask. At the interview, the leader will introduce the guest to the group and then ask him questions and let him answer them. Following the interview, the leader will moderate questions from individual group members addressed to the special guest. At the close, he will also summarize the information presented and suggest ways to use the information.

You can enrich the learning experience of the group if you make advance assignments for research and study in the area of information to be considered. This could take the form of preparing the questions to be asked during the interview.

Another form of interview consists of assigning different members of the group questions to ask of particular people during the week, and presenting their findings to the large group at the next meeting. For example, in a study of different religions, you could prepare a series of questions which your teens might ask their Roman Catholic or Jewish friends, depending on your unit of study. This creates more variety in response and gets more of your students actively involved in the learning process.

An interview across the miles can be arranged by using a tape recorder. A blank tape with a typed questionnaire could be sent to a missionary on the field or to denominational leaders at the headquarters office. The returned tape would provide the basis for an up-to-the-minute discussion.

FIELD TRIPS

Field trips provide firsthand information related to the topic being studied. This obviously takes more time than the Sunday morning session, unless the point of interest is nearby.

There is more involved in a profitable field trip experience than just going to the point of interest. The departmental learning leader should carefully make all the arrangements and spend time preparing the group members for the trip. The leader may prepare a statement of goals and objectives for the trip; provide relevant data about the place being visited; and distribute instructions regarding the details of the trip.

Following the field trip, the learning leader will evaluate the experience with the group members, summarizing and applying any important points of interpretation regarding what was observed.

For example, a group of junior highs were studying the resurrection of believers. The discussion focused on the meaning of death for the Christian. The youth minister, who was the large group learning leader, suggested that the group visit a mortuary.

Arrangements were made with the mortician, who was also a Christian, for a visit to the mortuary. He agreed to speak to the group, explaining his work and ministry. Following the visit, the youth minister led an evaluation session about individual reactions to the trip. The combination of study before the field trip and evaluation following the trip made it a very positive learning experience.

A group of senior high youths were studying the Roman Catholic religion. Following the study of the Mass, it was suggested that they go as a group with the teacher to an early Mass the next Sunday morning. This time they were passive observers, whereas the junior highs had opportunity to ask questions. Following the Mass, the senior high group went to a nearby restaurant for their evaluation session and breakfast, returning to church in time for the worship service. The purpose of the field trip, to the teacher, was to illustrate what they had been studying. But in conversation later, it appeared that the biggest value of the field trip was to demonstrate the obvious differences between the Mass and their own tradition.

The careful use of this method will add to your study units. The field trips described above were taken only after careful planning, which included a provision for evaluation sessions immediately following the field trip.

LECTURE

In a recent survey, the question was asked: "In your opinion which is the poorest method of teaching?" Ironically most responded by saying that the lecture is the poorest, yet continued to rely almost exclusively on lecturing in their class. While it is true that the lecture is unfortunately the overused standby of the Sunday school teacher, it can be an exciting and interesting teaching method. Any method is poor if used incorrectly or too often.

At the *Familiarization* stage in the learning process, basic information is presented. The lecture is probably the quickest, most efficient way to present this information. However, the lecture is probably one of the most difficult of all teaching methods to use effectively with youth. As the diagram shows, the communication is one-way; from the teacher to the learner. The entire burden rests on the teacher. He has done the preparation and now he does the talking. Since the student is passive, the learning leader must be dynamic, informative and interesting.

Just because the teacher presents a certain amount of material does not guarantee that the learner either hears or understands what is being presented. This is why it is recommended that the lecture be used in combination with other methods which will move the learner from a passive role to a more active involvement in the learning process.

When working with junior high youth, the lecture should be no longer than ten minutes, followed by student-involving methods, such as buzz groups, roleplay, questions and answer. Older teens can take longer lecture periods, but these should not go beyond 15 minutes without some time for involvement or response from the group members.

When using the lecture method, the lecturer should keep in mind certain principles:

Know your subject, organizing the material into a teaching outline that makes sense to you. Lecturing is *not* parroting the teacher's manual, even though it may be written in a conversational style. The teacher's manual is a resource to help you organize and present the material in your own style.

As you lecture, keep in mind the lesson objectives which you have prepared. They should help you keep in mind the organization of the material.

Maintain eye contact with your students. Know the material well enough so that you do not need to keep referring to your notes. Eye contact will help you hold the students' interest, and will also provide you with clues on how they are reacting to your presentation.

Listen to your voice; avoid the dull monotone that puts an audience to sleep, especially on a Sunday morning. Maintain a good pace in speaking. Talking too slowly gets dull, and talking too fast will lose parts of your audience.

Try to maintain a conversational style. Be relaxed and informal in your presentation, avoiding extremes. Share with your students some of your feelings during the preparation of the lesson, along with some of the questions and concerns you had or still have. This glimpse into your own feelings helps the student feel involved in the process and helps hold his interest.

Two methods that will help vary the lecture and get the learners participating are word association and define-a-word. In word association, the teacher explains that he is going to say a word, and he wants the students to remember the first thing that comes to mind. He then says the word—such as *witness, forgiveness, family*—and calls on volunteers to give their responses. This leads to further discussion of the concept.

In define-a-word, the leader simply asks for volunteers to define a particular word.

Finally, and perhaps most important—*use visual aids!* Visual aids are not just for preschoolers and primary children. Studies by Zuck and Getz show that one of the biggest complaints of youth against Bible teachers is that they do not use enough visual aids.[1] In fact, it appears that the need for visual aids increases, rather than decreases, with youth and adults. Youth and adults have the highest retention level when visual aids are used.

CHALKBOARD: This is probably the most available and most used visual aid. Usually the lecturer makes notations during the lecture to underscore what he is saying. Or he might diagram or illustrate a point being made.

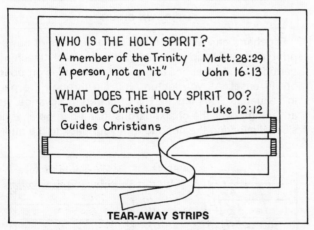

TEAR-AWAY STRIPS

Advance preparation of the chalkboard increases its effectiveness. One method turns the chalkboard into a "progressive disclosure" chart. This involves writing your points on the chalkboard, using one line for each point. These are covered with adding machine tape or some other kind of paper strip, attached with a piece of tape. These strips are torn off as you progress through the lecture.

FLIPCHARTS: There are several types. The flip-down chart is illustrated in Figure H, and is especially effective with youth. Lettering is done on both sides of strips of heavy paper or light cardboard. These are attached to poster boards or chalkboard, leaving space between the strips equal to their width. One side gives a word or phrase and the other side gives the definition or application. These are flipped down to reveal the points as you move through the lecture.

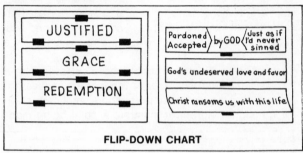

FLIP-DOWN CHART

Flipcharts can also be made on large pads of newsprint with a felt tip pen. Or you can attach teaching cartoons or illustrations to one pad. The pad is propped on an easel. As you lecture you flip through the pad in sequence. This flipchart is prepared in advance. Its advantage over the chalkboard is that it can be at your side, eliminating the need to turn your back to the audience.

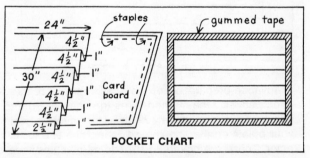

POCKET CHART

The pocket chart shown in Figure 1 has pockets in which word cards or other visuals are placed. The cards are easy to put in, remove, or move around.

MAPS: Not all maps have to be hung on a wall. You might suspend a globe in the middle of the room, or tape the map to the floor with chairs arranged around it. Or you might outline the map on the floor with chalk and group chairs on the map according to cities. You might also use a relief map, created by a work group for a project.

OVERHEAD PROJECTOR: You may not be familiar with an overhead projector, but your students will be. Overhead projectors are used daily in public education. They project transparencies over the shoulder of the speaker to a screen or blank wall. The lecturer can use transparencies prepared before the session, or he can use special marker pens to write on a transparency as he might on the chalkboard. The speaker never turns away from the audience, maintaining eye contact with the students. By turning the projector off, he changes the focus of the students' attention from the screen back to himself, adding variety of attention points.

You will find the overhead projector one of the most versatile teaching tools available today for use with larger groups. Cost is usually not prohibitive. Each departmental learning leader in the youth division should have an overhead projector. Instructions about use of the overhead projector are available from the dealers who sell them.

LISTENING TEAMS

The large group is divided into special teams to listen for an answer to a specific question. The departmental learning leader will give specific assignments to each team to keep in mind as they view a film, listen to a lecture or panel, watch a roleplay or drama or listen to a musical presentation. The assignment may be the same for all groups, or may be different for each group.

The listening teams may meet after the presentation to discuss their response before presenting it to the whole group. Or they may respond individually.

The room arrangement will help set up the listening team; arrange the chairs into as many groups as there will be teams. Make sure the assignments are clear before proceeding with the presentation.

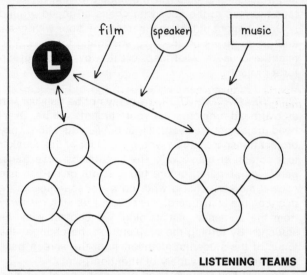

film speaker music

L

LISTENING TEAMS

This method works with any kind of presentation that involves a large group listening to something for a period of time. It can set the stage for good discussion, or even for an informal debate, if there are two listening teams.

RESEARCH AND REPORT

There are several ways to use this method. One is to give individual research assignments to be carried out between class sessions.

The assignment can range from a series of interviews to a study of books and periodicals. Or an individual might be assigned to visit an institution to learn how the youth can be involved in service there.

When planning individual assignments, the problem is presented to the group; then specific assignments are given to individual members. The time (usually the next meeting) is specified for reporting the results of the research.

Another variation involves giving assignments to small groups or teams. These are researched during the week, or possibly during the class session. The latter possibility would require the departmental leaders to have resource materials available in the classroom.

For example, the class might come to a passage of Scripture with several possible interpretations. The class is divided into research teams, each given several commentaries and Bible dictionaries. Each team is given an assignment which they research. After time for study, small groups are reconvened into the large group and reports are given by each research team. The departmental learning leader summarizes the results of the reports.

Another variation is the *book report*. Related novels or biographies are assigned to different individuals, who give a report to the large group at the appropriate time in the unit study.

Listening teams can be used for audience involvement during the report sessions.

ROLEPLAY

This is a special type of drama which is especially effective with youth. A roleplay is a brief, unrehearsed presentation of a real-life situation by two or three students while the rest of the group observes. This method especially deals with the "feeling" area of learning.

First a problem is presented to the group. It might be an open-end story with the ending to be acted out, a biblical story or a modern parallel to a biblical situation.

Once the problem is presented, actors are chosen. Care must be exercised in not giving an unpopular person the unpopular role. Names are given the actors, and some brief instructions could be given either individually or to the group of actors. There is no rehearsal, but a few moments are given to allow the actors time to "psych" themselves up for the role.

The actual roleplay should not be too long, running from one to ten minutes. The number of participants should seldom be more than three; two is ideal. It is the learning leader's responsibility to make sure each actor knows what is expected of him in his role.

In the parable of the prodigal son, the learning leader might focus on the attitude of the elder brother. After describing his bitterness and self-pity, three "actors" would be chosen, one to play the part of the father, one the prodigal, and the other the elder son. The setting would be the next day, when the two brothers meet.

From that point on, the "actors" are on their own. The conversation is imaginary, but helps the learners get into the feelings of the characters. Perhaps the father could interrupt their conversation, relating his feelings on the matter.

Another example is a problem between a son and his father. The father could be letting the son have both barrels in an argument over the use of the car. This might be done twice, reversing the roles the second time.

Following the presentation, the group discusses what has been acted out and suggests strengths and weaknesses in the solutions presented. If there is interest, the scene might be repeated with different actors involved.

The evaluation should include debriefing the actors, asking them why they did what they did and how they felt about their role. Listening teams might be assigned to "feel with" an individual actor and to be prepared to discuss why they reacted as they did in the roleplay. During evaluation and discussion, the assigned names should be used rather than the person's real name.

The leader stops the roleplay when the point has been made and emotions are still actively involved. The roleplay should not continue beyond the climatic point of the situation.

Another way to use roleplay is to divide the class into two or three groups and have each group represent one of the actors. They do not act out the situation, but attempt to feel how the person might have felt and then give reasons for acting as they did.

For example, in the parable of the good Samaritan, one group would represent the priest, another group would be the Levite, and the third group would be the good Samaritan. Individual members of each group are then asked to explain why they behaved as they did in the parable.

This method has tremendous value when used correctly and with a clear objective in mind. A great deal of Christian truth involves relationships—how we are to treat one another because we know and love God through Jesus Christ. Roleplay deals with relationships, and can help apply, crystallize and bring to life spiritual principles as no other method can.

SYMPOSIUM

This is a series of speeches presented to the large group on different phases of the material being studied. The speeches could be the results of several research projects.

As you see in the diagram, the material is presented by the speakers without any interaction between speakers or between the speakers and audience. This method is valuable at the *Familiarization* level of the learning process, where basic information is presented.

The speakers could either be special resource people brought in for the symposium, or members of the group who have prepared special reports. Symposiums work nicely with listening teams and are usually followed either by buzz groups or by class sessions with discussion.

PANELS

The panel differs from the symposium in that the resource speakers actually converse together. Three to six people discuss topics or questions under the guidance of the departmental learning leader or other moderator.

Sometimes a panel discussion will follow a symposium presentation. Questions can come from other panel members, from the moderator, or from the audience. The moderator does not contribute to the discussion, but seeks to involve each of the panel members.

In both cases, the departmental learning leader needs to clarify the issue being discussed. He also selects the panel members or symposium speakers and meets with them before the meeting to be sure they understand the procedure and have prepared adequately. As moderator, he will summarize the major contributions of the panelists and suggest further opportunity for discussion of the issue.

You now have a basic portfolio of methods which can

be used with youth. You need one further suggestion, which is technically not a method, but *is* an important part of being a learning leader: you need to become an expert on resources.

This means that when you do not know the answers, you do know where the solutions might be found. You are aware of the available books that relate to certain problem areas for youth. You build a library of books you can use or lend to others. This does not mean you have to read everything available, but you should know what Christian books are available that speak to the needs and problems of today's youth.

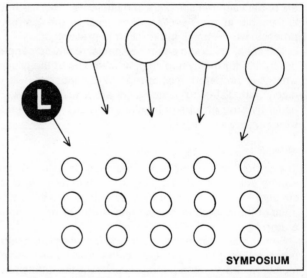

SYMPOSIUM

You also need to know resource people. Build a list of possible speakers and their areas of specialty. Know what people are available when you need to call for help. If a particular subject or problem is beyond your ability, who can you ask to give assistance? Youth need learning leaders who care enough to keep on learning themselves, and who are humble enough to ask for help when needed.

God help us to be sensitive to the leading of His Spirit as we seek to lead youth into responsible Christian commitment and growth, growing up together in Christ!

FOOTNOTES

CHAPTER 7

1 • Martha M. Leypoldt, *40 Ways to Teach in Groups* (Valley Forge: Judson Press, 1967), p. 17.
2 • Sara Little, *Learning Together in the Christian Fellowship* (Richmond: John Knox Press, 1956), p. 33.
3 • Edgar Dale, *Audio-Visual Methods in Teaching* (The Dryden Press. Revised 1954), p. 43.
4 • Leypoldt, *40 Ways to Teach in Groups,* adapted from p. 27.

CHAPTER 8

1 • Ron R. Ritchie, *A Proposed Program for the Development of Spiritual Gifts in the Local Church* (from an unpublished thesis, Dallas Theological Seminary).
2 • Little, *Learning Together in the Christian Fellowship,* p. 38.
3 • Lyman Coleman, *Acts Alive, Man Alive,* and *Kaleidoscope* (Newton, Pennsylvania: Halfway House), for examples of these creative drawing methods.
4 • Acts 10:13, *New American Standard Bible* (La Habra, Calif.: Foundation Press) © 1971 by The Lockman Foundation.
5 • For further guidance in using the inductive method of study in teaching or in your own life, see Oletta Wald's book *Joy of Discovery* (Minneapolis: Bible Banner Press, 1956).
6 • Leypoldt, *40 Ways to Teach in Groups,* p. 92.

CHAPTER 9

1 • Roy B. Zuck and A. Gene Getz, *Christian Youth: An In-depth Study* (Chicago: Moody Press, 1968), p. 89.

BIBLIOGRAPHY

Benson, Dennis. *The Now Generation.*
Richmond: John Knox Press, 1969.

Bowman, Locke E., Jr. *Straight Talk About Teaching in Today's Church.* Philadelphia: Westminster, 1967.

Burton, Janet. *Guiding Youth.*
Nashville: Convention Press, 1969.

Duvall, Evelyn M. *Today's Teen-Agers.*
New York: Association Press, 1966.

Erikson, Erik H. *Identity: Youth and Crisis.*
New York: W. W. Norton and Co. 1968.

Ezell, Mancil. *Youth in Bible Study/New Dynamics.*
Nashville: Convention Press, 1970.

Gesell, Arnold, Ilg, Frances L., and Ames, Louise Bates. *Youth: The Years from Ten to Sixteen.*
New York: Harper and Brothers, 1956.

Joy, Donald M. *Meaningful Learning in the Church.*
Winona Lake: Light and Life Press, 1969.

Leonard, George B. *Education and Ecstasy.*
New York: Delacorte Press, 1968.

Leypoldt, Martha M. *40 Ways to Teach in Groups.*
Valley Forge: Judson Press, 1967.

Little, Sara. *Learning Together in the Christian Fellowship.*
Richmond: John Knox Press, 1956.

McBurney, James H. and Mills, G. E. *Argumentation and Debate.* New York: Macmillan, 1964.

McLuhan, Marshall. *Understanding Media: The Extensions of Man.* New York: McGraw-Hill Book Co., 1964.

Mead, Margaret. *Culture and Commitment.*
New York: Doubleday and Co., 1970.

Murphree, T. Garvice and Dorothy. *Understanding Youth.*
Nashville: Convention Press, 1969.

Rogers, Carl R. *Freedom to Learn.*
Columbus: Charles E. Merrill Pub. Co., 1969.

Schaeffer, Francis A. *The God Who Is There.*
Downers Grove, Ill.: Inter-Varsity Press, 1968.

Sisemore, John T. *Blueprint for Teaching.*
Nashville: Broadman Press, 1964.

Snyder, Ross. *Youth and Their Culture.*
Nashville: Abingdon, 1969.

Stewart, Charles W. *Adolescent Religion.*
Nashville: Abingdon, 1967.

Strang, Ruth. *The Adolescent Views Himself.*
New York: McGraw-Hill Book Co., 1957.

Strommen, Merton P. *Profiles of Church Youth.*
St. Louis: Concordia Publishing House, 1963.

Wald, Oletta. *The Joy of Discovery.*
Minneapolis: Bible Banner Press, 1956.

Zuck, Roy B., and Getz, A. Gene. *Christian Youth: An In-Depth
Study.* Chicago: Moody Press, 1968.

Zuck, Roy B. *The Holy Spirit in Your Teaching.*
Wheaton: Scripture Press Publications, 1968.

𝕿rain for 𝕰ffective Leadership

The impact of effective leadership can be felt in every area of your Sunday school. Train your leaders and teachers with **Success Handbooks** from ICL. Prepared by recognized authorities in Christian education, the handbooks in each series are especially designed for four basic age groups:
Early Childhood, Children, Youth, Adult.

Series 1, Ways to Help Them Learn
The Success Handbook on each level discusses the learning process, age characteristics, needs and abilities, plus proven teaching techniques.

Series 2, Ways to Plan and Organize Your Sunday School
The Success Handbook on each level offers guidance in building your Sunday school with a plan consistent and effective at every level.

Each Success Handbook $1.95.
Boxed set of all 8: $14.95.

Regal Books
Glendale, California